Practical steps to lead you out of the wilderness and into the promised land.

Wilderness Mentality

Stop Your Stinkin' Thinkin'

Stephanie Rene Reck LMSW, LBT, BCCC

ISBN: 1-4802-3151-7
ISBN-13: 9781480231511

Dedication:

Dedicated to my husband, Stephen, without him I could never have finished this book. Thank you, my love for your support and encouragement. You are truly a man after God's own heart.

To my son, Jonathon, whom I love and believe God has awesome things for. Thank you Jesus, for saving my life and redeeming me to wholeness and purpose.

Table of Contents

"Change your thoughts and you change your world."
Norman Vincent Peale

Introduction: Woe is me. That is the story of my life. Ever heard of the glass half empty thinking? Well that was me, always blaming my poor, pitiful life on my circumstances. Yes, I endured hardships of all sorts. I have been abused, abandoned, rejected, depressed, lonely, addicted and many more things. I never realized that my circumstances were affecting my attitude. I was hardly ever content and wished for a different existence. I thought everyone else's life was blessed but mine. I felt my life was one big punishment.

Now this book is not for the weak, but if you want to get real and examine your life through the eyes of Christ, then this is the right book for you. Just don't read the book, but apply what you have learned.

Through many years of being discontent, I entered into what I like to describe as "wilderness thinking." My mind was a mess. What happened? I became anxious, depressed, fearful, worried, a complainer, a fault-finder, critical and coveted other's lives. I became thankless and ungrateful. If I can be real, I was even angry at God! Did He not know I wanted the house with the white-picket fence plus 2.5 well-behaved and loving children?

Years of stinkin' thinkin' over my life led me into the wilderness, and in the wilderness I stayed for years. I tried everything to "get happy." Don't get me wrong, I was saved, a believer in the Lord, Jesus Christ, but I was not free. Can anyone relate to this? Are you a believer but living in bondage to your thoughts and circumstances? God had to do some clean-up in my mind and restore to me a freedom I did not know.

I was instantly saved at 24 years old, but not instantly delivered from my mind, my thinking, and my rotten attitude. I had certain expectations of my life and they were not being fulfilled. I had unmet longings and desires that were seemingly going unnoticed. I did not sign-up for the tragedies and pitfalls of my life. I thought God was punishing me for the years I lived in rebellion. My thinking about my life just plain stunk. It was rotten. I needed an overhaul in my thinking.

This book comprises years of my journey and what God has showed me and taught me. I use my background in social work and counseling as well as current research. This book is a combination of what God has shared with me personally through my years of journal writings and Bible study and my education and research into this area. I have a lot more personal experience in this area than I would like to say. I battled many heartaches and trials before completing this book.

I can personally attest to everything given in this book because I have lived it and worked through it. God had me write this book not just for you, but for me as well. I do stand on the authorative Word of God as my source in writing this book. So come along with me on this journey. If you feel you have been dealt a bad hand in life, I understand, but God loves you too much to keep you in such despair. Open your heart, open your mind and receive what God has for you.

In His grace,
Stephanie

Very important please read before reading this book.

preface: Before beginning on this journey together, it is important that if you do not have a personal relationship with the Lord and Savior, Jesus Christ, or if you might need to rededicate your life to Him, that we take this time right now to get right with God.

So do you know where you are going when you die? You might say, "Heaven or I will go to heaven because my family believed in God." So how do you really know that you are going to heaven to live in eternity with God? Have you personally, not your family, asked Jesus to be your Lord and Savior? Have you known God, but walked away from Him or stopped believing in Him somewhere along your walk? Let us not go on another day without getting right before God. If you are not a Christian or you are not certain if you even believe, ask God to show you who He is and what He did for you. Stop now and ask. After He responds to you, let's pray the prayer of salvation. Salvation means you are right with God, He has forgiven you and taken away all of your sins. He also has given you His spirit to dwell in you to help you and He has given you eternal life with Him in the heavens. God says, "If you confess with your mouth that you believe I am the Son of God, you shall be saved." (Paraphrase Romans 10:9)

Let's pray the Salvation prayer together or rededicate your life back to Jesus:
Heavenly Father,

I believe that you are the Son of God. I believe you rose from the dead on the third day to give me life. I believe that you were born of the virgin Mary and lived as a human and died a sinless life as a sacrifice for me. God, forgive me of all of my sins and come into my life.

I invite you Lord into my life to change me. Thank you for dying on the cross for me.
In your name Jesus I pray.

If you just prayed the pray of Salvation, congratulations the angels in heaven are rejoicing over your Salvation, and all of your sins have been washed away. Welcome, dear sister or brother in Christ. You will now know for certain that you will be in heaven for eternity with Jesus. Your life will begin to change, not in a bad way, but in a very amazing way. It will be a journey like you have never been on before. Your life will be radically changed. Take it from me, a former alcohol and drug abuser, a teenage mom, a heavy partier and nightclub "queen", and a former dabbler in most religions and I even had a period of complete non-belief in God (I guess some would say, Atheist).

If you made this decision today, then write it down with the date.

Today, I,

_____

received Salvation on this day of:_____.

There are some very important things to do now that you are a believer in Christ. Not a religious person, but a person who is a Christian, which means you have a personal relationship with Christ. This is not about religion, but about a relationship. Just because you go to church or call yourself a Christian, does not necessarily mean you are one. If you sit in a garage, does that now make you a car?

What are your next steps now:

I. Get a good Bible, one that you can understand. Go to a Christian bookstore and tell someone you need help finding a good Bible and that you are a new believer. I have several different versions of the Bible, so that I can understand the Bible better.

2. Get on a Bible reading plan. Download a 30 day, 60 day or yearly Bible reading plan. You can find these anywhere and usually for free. Search the internet for Bible reading plans.

3. Find a good Bible-believing church to start attending. Make sure you feel God's presence where you attend and that there is freedom there. That it is not a church that has religious bondage. That means no burdens and extra rules. You should enjoy the church you attend, but you should also feel some conviction from the Holy Spirit, not condemnation. If you attend a church and it is "feel-good messages" or pop psychology, then find one with a good balance. It should not be fire and brimstone messages every week or "feel good" messages every week either.

4. Spend daily time with God. Meditate on his Word and get a journal and begin to record what He shows you. Also, write praises, prayers and the date on each thing you write. That way you can go back and look at the dates and say," God intervened here or I am making progress."

5. Pray daily and at all times. Not some sort of ritual, but God says in His Word, " to pray without ceasing." He also says to pray about everything. Don't know how to pray?, It's really simple, talk to God like He is your best friend. Tell Him everything: your worries, your fears, your hopes and what you are thankful for, today. Start your prayers and end your prayers with thanksgiving and praise. Enter His "courts" with thanksgiving and praise. End your prayers with, in Jesus name. Why? because His name has power.

Chapter I
The Habit of Positive Thinking

Norman Vincent Peale was the first author who linked positive thinking and Christianity. He has authored the incredibly powerful book, *The Power of Positive Thinking.* In Peale's audio book he says, "If you want to change your circumstances you must start thinking differently." The author, recommends developing faith in God to overcome lack of self-confidence, and to do this through prayer and scripture. We know that positive thoughts alone will not change our thinking, but if you couple God's Word with your thoughts then real change can occur. I used to believe that positive thinking alone was sufficient, but without the truth of God's word, true change on your own attempt is futile.

The experts say it generally takes between 21 and 30 days to break a habit or start a new one. Generally speaking most habits can be broken in that time frame, but sometimes it does go beyond the 21-30 day rule. If you're trying to break the habit of negative thinking, develop a plan for 30 days and then reevaluate at the end of the 30 days. Goals are more manageable if you break them off in 30 day chunks. Don't get discouraged if you have to repeat the goal.

Remember, the enemy does not want you to break through and you have had many years to form these negative mental habits. Keep in mind, the first couple of days of forming your new habit will be met with enthusiasm but around the second week, that enthusiasm wears off and it gets a bit more difficult. Keep going, press in and you will feel exhilarated in the last week, however, if you do not achieve your goal of getting rid of negative thoughts, then try again. Failure is only giving up, not trying.

"Finally brethren, whatever things are true, whatever things are noble, whatever things are just, whatever things are pure, whatever things are lovely, whatever things are of good report, if there is any virtue and if there is anything praiseworthy-meditate on these things."

Philippians 4:8-9, NKJV

Where are your thoughts? Are they lining up with the above scripture? Be aware of your thoughts; don't just allow anything to fall into your head. The battlefield is really in the mind. A great book to read about that topic is, Joyce Meyer's, *"Battlefield of the Mind."* This battlefield has been going on since the days of Adam and Eve.

Look at Genesis 3, here in this chapter we see Satan tempting Eve with, "Did God really say that…?" (Paraphrase). Instead of Eve taking every thought captive, she chose to believe the lies of Satan. When we believe lies over the truth of God's word we fall prey to our minds coming under Satan's control. Satan's plan is to cause doubt, discouragement, diversion, defeat, and delay. However, these plans start in the mind first. Satan plants a "seed" of doubt, and we choose to water the "seed" by not taking that thought captive into the obedience of Christ. So when you're making your 21 to 30 day plan to change your thinking, never, leave God's truth out. It is not sufficient alone to fight the battle of your thoughts on your own. If you don't know the truth of God's word, you will never be free.

Have a daily devotional time with God, preferably first thing in the morning when your thoughts are the most defeating. Have you ever noticed that when you get up in the morning, the battle in your mind rages? So make it a daily practice to spend time in God's word. Write scripture that speaks to you on index cards and memorize and place the cards all through your house. I have index cards in my house everywhere as a reminder of God's truth. Pick a chapter out of the Bible to read at a time; try not to randomly read anywhere. If you're new to reading God's word, try a monthly or yearly Bible reading plan. Search a monthly or yearly Bible reading plan and you will surely find one to help you. Some days you may not feel like reading the Bible or spending time with the Lord, but I encourage you to press on anyway. You always come out better when you have spent time in the Lord's presence.

When negative thoughts come, and they will, you need not fight them, but replace them with positive ones. That is why it is important to know God's truth, so you can replace the negative thought with a positive, faith-filled statement. Here is an example: "I am a worthless human being." Instead you could say, "I am not a worthless human being, I am a child of God and I have been created for a purpose." It will take practice, but if you continue, you will see the results of speaking positive, faith-filled statements.

Another thing you could do is make a list of positive, faith-filled affirmations about yourself and read them daily over yourself. Examples of these affirmations would be: I am a child of God, I am more than victorious though Christ Jesus, I can do all things through Christ who strengthens me. Make your own affirmations, but line the affirmations with God's truth. Say the affirmations you make in the morning and before you go to bed at night. (see appendix A)

In an article entitled, *What is Positive Thinking?* by Kendra Cherry she discussed that one might be tempted to assume that positive thinking implies seeing the world through rose-colored lenses by ignoring or glossing over the negative aspects of life. However, she notes that positive thinking actually means approaching life's challenges with a positive outlook. It does not necessarily mean avoiding or ignoring the bad things; instead it involves making the most of potentially bad situations, trying to see the best in people and viewing yourself and your abilities in a positive light.

It is not our circumstances that defeat us but our minds. It is what we think about our circumstances that we can be overcomers or defeated. Everything starts with a thought. If you think your circumstance is overwhelming, guess what, you will begin to feel overwhelmed. Our feelings are generated by our thinking. Do you want to feel better? Then what are you saying to yourself? Are you saying, "I'm a loser, I'm a failure?" Eventually you will begin to believe that lie, if you do not replace those lies with the truth. So here is another example of how you could do that: "I may have failed a couple of times but that does not make me a loser, God is for me and His plans are good for me." It is not easy to change ingrained patterns of thinking, but in time you will achieve having the thought life God intends you to have. For me it was a process, my negative thinking patterns were not immediately done away with, but I was determined to not give up until I was thinking more like Christ. Yes, it may be a battle, but we know that anytime we as Christians try to be delivered from something, the enemy does not like that. I say, do it anyway, because we are more than conquerors!

"Formulate and stamp indelibly on your mind a mental picture of yourself succeeding. Hold this picture tenaciously. Never permit it to fade. Your mind will seek to develop the picture. . . .Do not build obstacles in your imagination."

Norman Vincent Peale

Can we change our circumstances? Usually not, but we can change our thoughts about our circumstances. It is not our circumstances that change us; it's our attitude towards them. Our thoughts are usually automatic, but we can choose to stop our negative thoughts and replace with the truth of God's word. Not everything that enters our minds are we supposed to accept. What does God's word say about what comes into our minds?, let's look at this scripture:

"And do not be conformed to this world, but be transformed by the renewing of your mind, that you may prove what is that good and acceptable and perfect will of God."
                                                                    Romans 12:2 NKJV

Here is what the Message Bible says, *don't become so well-adjusted to your culture that you fit into it without even thinking. Instead fix your attention on God. You'll be changed from the inside out. Readily recognize what he wants from you, and quickly respond to it. Unlike the culture around you, always dragging you down to its level of immaturity, God brings the best out of you, develops well-formed maturity in you.*
So to sum up that scripture, stop being like everybody else. Look around, most people are not faith-filled, but whiners and complainers. Now I am not being harsh when I say that, I myself have endured countless hardships and trials that would knock out the best in anyone. I have tried to complain about my circumstances, such as, "That's not fair", or "why me?" I had become angry and even jealous of others at times. A good book to read in the Bible, if you have not already, is the book of Job. I recommend reading the entire book. Here is a man who literally lost everything, and yes still choose to trust and praise God. Sure he had a moment or two, but the point is he got up despite his circumstances. That is what I am telling you, get up, and stop saying things that are negative. I am not saying, you cannot have a moment to process, but then turn it around. My life verse is Romans 8:28, which states that, " God works ALL things out for our good for those who love Him and are called according to His purposes." There is a very good reason that is my life verse. Throughout this book, I am sharing parts of my testimony with you. Not to relive or rehash, but so that our God will receive the glory for everything I endured.
I had my son when I was a mere 16 years old. It was such a struggle, but even in my heathen years (I call those years' heathen before I was saved), I knew it could not get any worse. Well I was wrong, after giving birth to my son, everything came spiraling down. The father of my son decides he was not cut out to be a father and we parted ways. I got saved several years later and married a wonderful Godly man. All is perfect in perfect land, right? Not really. What do you do when your teenage son is getting involved in drugs and that

eventually leads him to an almost year stay at Teen Challenge? Teen Challenge is a Christ-centered addiction recovery program. Well, I learned my thoughts played a big role in my emotional state. I spiraled down into a depression; I know it was directly related to my thoughts. You know what you eventually think about will produce a feeling. So here are some examples of my thinking at the time: " I know he is going to end up like everyone else in my family," and "I don't want to show my face, I will just lie in bed all day." Eventually I began to feel what I was thinking. I was not taking every thought captive into the obedience of Christ. I was listening to the lies of the enemy, and believing them. I was not focusing on faith and God's promises, but on my circumstances. I took my eyes off of Jesus and to my problems. I will have more to say about my son later in the book, because that trial turned into another trail, which led me, deeper in the wilderness.

Our thoughts are powerful, I had no idea I was making my problem bigger and unmanageable by the words I was speaking. Why do we do that? Sometimes our minds are conditioned to think negatively. Think of how you were brought up, how were problems handled, stress and conflict handled? Was it wrought with worry, fear, anxiousness or maybe even anger? I experienced all of those things growing up. I was raised in a very negative environment. So hence, I learned how to be negative. My family was not a family to say, lets pray about that or to say something positive about a situation. I grew up in the family that viewed the cup half empty and not half full. Can you relate? Go back and see where the root of your thinking stemmed from in your life. It is important to know, so that you can replace the lies with the truth of God's word. My mind became conditioned to negativity, pessimism, worry, fear and anxiousness. My mind was a mess; it was all over the place. I felt I had absolutely no control in my thinking and I was in serious bondage with my thinking. I was just defeated, depressed, and discouraged. Been there? What a mess my mind was in, so I tried everything to cure my mind. I thought I would try alcohol, drugs, and prescription medications. None all these worked for me. I did find that I needed more of these substances and developed myself some nasty addictions. I tried counseling, but it did not work for me because I did not do what the counselor told me to do. Now I am a counselor, so I am not discrediting counseling, I am saying that if you go, you must do the work. Changing any behavior including our thoughts, takes work. As a side note, I do believe in the miraculous healing of our Lord and Savior, but for most of us we have to work through our problems. I like to say we are being refined by the refiner's fire. Who is the refiner? Jesus Christ. Why does He refine us? To make us into His image.

If our thoughts are faithless than our heavenly father is not pleased. God is pleased when we are faithful and when we speak faith-filled words over our circumstances. It is by faith that we can move mountains, but if you're speaking defeat over your problems then you are probably not moving any mountains.

Do you want to remain in you condition or do you want to be healed? Than get up and be healed of your thinking today. Start today as day #1, and if you fail, than get up again. Try again and try as many times as it takes. I cannot tell you how many times it finally took me to change my thinking, so many times there are too many to count. What you must have is unbelievable determination that God and you can do the seemingly impossible.

> Some people have an inborn tendency to be negative; others become negative because of the barrage of depressing news listened to daily. What are you listening to and watching every day? It will affect your thinking. Others have a negative sense of self-worth that could stem from our past experiences, such as failure. According to experts, negativity actually impedes impulses from being transmitted between the central nervous system and the brain. Because the brain cannot interpret impulses correctly, this affects the functioning of the brain and body. Memory is affected; sleep disturbances are experienced; emotional upsets become the order of the day; and immune function can also be affected, resulting in susceptibility to colds and flu. According to a recent study undertaken by the department of Public Health Sciences in Sweden, women who expressed their anger had a 42% chance of dying from heart complications versus the 19% of women who suppressed or controlled their anger. Learning to channel negative emotions diminishes strain and helps the body cope better with trying situations.(Hupston, 2010).

According to Hupston, it will take time and effort to control negative thoughts. We know as Christians we can do nothing on our own strength and merit. She discusses being aware of your thinking patterns and to make a conscious effort to replace negative thoughts with positive thoughts. Basically replacing the lies or distorted thinking we have that the enemy throws our way with the truth of God's word.

Write on index cards the scripture that deals with the issues you are facing, and place all through your home or take them with you and read the cards throughout the day. An example would be if you have trouble with anxiety, look up scriptures that deal with anxiety, such as:

"Don't fret or worry, instead of worrying, pray. Let petitions and praises shape your worries into prayers, letting God know your concerns."

Philippians 4:6 MSG

That is how you begin to replace those negative thoughts. If you don't replace those negative thoughts, you will have an empty, passive mind. This is ground for the enemy to operate, a passive mind. Hupston also discusses staying away from "emotional vampires" and other negative people. What is an emotional vampire? Someone who "sucks" the life out of you, you know the type; we have all had friends like them. You end up leaving drained and worn out. Be aware of who your hanging out with, if your hanging out with folks who are negative, chances are you will be too!

Did your mother ever tell you, birds of a feather flock together? Well she was right; you are who you hang out with. But you say, they are family or I am ministering to them. If they're pulling you down and you are around them frequently, chances are their going to affect you. A good book to read if you're having trouble understanding this is, *Boundaries* by Drs. Cloud & Townsend. You can find this book at most Christian bookstores or online. It is a must read if you are dealing with these types of people. We all need healthy boundaries with people, and yes even our family, friends and people who we are ministering to.

Use positive affirmations with scriptures to help you deal with negative emotions. What defines a negative emotion? Worry, fear, anxiety, insecurity, depression, and anger. Negative reactions are complaining, judgmental, gossiping and criticism. Have any of these? Get rid of them, otherwise, you will stay in the wilderness. Read the book in the Bible, Exodus. The Israelites wandered in the desert for forty years because they decided to complain and not trust God.

Are you ready for the Promised Land?

"Positive thinking will let you do everything better than negative thinking will."

Zig Ziglar

Chapter 2
So What is Wilderness Thinking?

What is wilderness thinking? Not entering God's rest and trusting God's perfect will for our lives. We begin to look at our lives, our circumstances and begin to complain and get negative about our situations. We stop trusting God and start looking at our circumstances as hopeless. We begin to live in defeat and not victory. We start to question God's timing and God's promises and His will for our lives. I am a journal writer, I don't know if you are, but I highly recommend it. Journal your thoughts, your progress, and what God says to you. Date every journal entry, so that you can go back and look at your progress and see where God has worked and answered prayers. Get a journal, it helps I have always recommended to my clients to keep a journal, I can't say diary because the men don't get into that. When I suggested to my husband to keep a journal, he thought that was cool, but he said a diary is for girls. Sorry guys they are really the same thing.

Here is an excerpt from one of my journal entries:
This was taken from 5/04/05:

I began to write a list out to help me with my thinking, here goes.:

1.   Slow down your pace
2.   Stop thinking so much
3.   Stop trying to figure things out
4.   Enjoy your life right where it is
5.   Find peace and comfort through God
6.   Your plans are being worked out, so relax
7.   Forgive yourself
8.   Keep doing good
9.   Stop every negative or anxious thought, it is not of God
10. Keep pressing on

11. Learn to enjoy everything you do
12. Spend time with God, it helps
13. Rise above these troubling waters and a blessing will await you.

At the time of writing that journal entry, we were going through infertility treatments and trying to become foster parents. Part of my journey, has been trusting God and my dream of having four children, and that it may not be His will for me. I was absolutely miserable during that time; I focused on what I did not have. Well I did have my son, but he was involved in drugs and he was very rebellious. I did not get to fulfill my nurturing with him because most days I felt distant and aloof from him. I did not know my own child. Can anyone relate, does anyone have a child or children who have struggled with addiction? It is a journey that is not for the faint-hearted. I wrote some other thoughts down from that journal entry. Take time to exercise, spend at least one hour with God daily, do not be ruled by your emotions, and let your mind rest-just shut it off.

Author Norman Vincent Peale has said let your mind do nothing for 15 minutes every day. Turn off your thinking for just 15 minutes and get quiet. Do you known that most of our minds never shut down? We are so bombarded by our thoughts that our mind wanders all over, but we need to recondition our minds.

Do not be so hard on yourself, allow yourself to make mistakes. Believe you are of value and worth. You were created for a purpose and a plan. Do not believe that God does not have anything for you to do or that you failed in the past, so don't try again. Get up again and keep trying. NEVER GIVE UP, I SAY NEVER GIVE UP. So it's hard, do it anyway. I only have gotten this way because I was sick and tired of being sick and tired. God says cast your cares on Him and He will work everything out. So why be worried and stressed over things you have no control over. Realize that you are in progress, and not to expect perfectionism. I fell into that trap, because I was a perfectionist. If I did not control my thoughts perfectly, I would give up. Don't do that, you will have slumps, but learn and get up again.

Here is another journal entry; this will show you the struggle when trying to change.

8/06/05:

You don't believe, you are double-minded which always sets you up for an attack. Stop being double-minded. Choose to believe and you will see wonderful results. Stop trying to solve your own problems, give them to me (God) and I will take care of them. After you give them to Me, stop worrying about them. You have to be obedient and when you're not the enemy can attack. Have joy and peace through Me and not in your circumstances. Be patient, you are being delivered one thing at a time. Make a choice today to be obedient, trust Me and believe Me. Be obedient and things will be given to you. Enjoy where you are right now. Relax through Me, knowing that I am taking care. It does not matter what is going on around you, it is not too big for me. I know everything and every problem. I can work out everything to the good. You cannot help anyone until you help yourself. Be content right where you are. Develop a relaxed, joyful spirit in the midst of all your circumstances. Make a choice to surrender everything! Do not fret or have anxieties about anything. I am with you always. If you are double-minded it causes frustration and confusion. Choose to believe and trust. Love Me. I know your inner thoughts and *I* know that you don't believe and don't trust Me. If you believe and trust Me, you won't have the problems that you do. Just try it and see if there is a difference. Crucify the flesh every day, you have the gifts of the Holy Spirit and when you don't have the gifts of the Holy Spirit, you need to crucify the flesh. Stop believing in emotions and feelings-they are of the flesh. Start obeying your Spirit. Read this every day until you understand and obey it.

Go ahead and try this, modify this to fit your name and read it daily until you understand and believe it. Say and write out until you believe, Jesus is with me, Jesus dwells in Me. If you're not enjoying your life, start now. It does not matter what happens in this life anyways. Life is just a vapor, here today, gone tomorrow.

So when will you begin to enter the Promised Land?
Promised Land thinking has nothing to do with our circumstances, but everything to do with our attitudes about our circumstances.

Dear Heavenly Father,
Help us Lord to be gentle, calm, sweet-spirited, patient, loving, giving, joyful and peaceful. Let His peace dwell in you. Help me to think about you Lord all day. Help me to stop being judgmental, suspicious, jealous, envious and to stop comparing myself to others. Help me to be happy for others and to

love everyone. Help me to follow your commandments and to have a peace that is beyond my understanding. Help me Lord to be an example to others, your light that shines brightly in this dark world. Help me Lord not to get upset over small and large things, help me to be easy going. Help me to encourage others as you would encourage others. Let me be the light Lord, let me serve you Lord. Help us Lord to be content in our present circumstances and with the plans you have for us. Not our will Father, but your will be done. Help us to be thankful for what we have and not for what we don't. Help us Lord to have a positive, faith-filled attitude about everything.

In Jesus powerful name I pray, amen.

> *"A sincere prayer brings wonderful results,"*
>
> *James 5:16.*

Praise is a powerful weapon to use against the enemy. Sing unto the Lord, you might say I don't feel like it, I say do it anyway. You will feel better when you are finished. Get your ears away from listening to all secular music, which all is not bad, but all is not all good either. Download some great Christian artist like Hillsong, Martha Munizzi, Juanita Bynum, Third Day, and Mercy Me and if you're adventurous try some Christian rap from Grits and Lacrae. I still like rap music so these artist are great for that.

> *"We can rejoice, too, when we run into trials, for we know they are good for us- they help us learn to endure. And endurance develops strength of character in us, and character strengths our confident expectation of salvation."*
>
> *Romans 5:3-4*

Wait for the Lord in confident expectation. Be joyful today, not when your circumstances are perfect. Enjoy your life now. I have had some people say I reminded them of Joel Osteen, but they did not like that because he was too positive. Listen precious people of God, there will always be a critic, Get over it! I would rather be positive and victorious, then negative and defeated. Have you ever been around a negative person? They are not fun to be around, I know I use to be one. To be honest, I did not like being around myself either. How can you be too positive? One might say that is not realistic, and I say being faithless, negative is? I am not saying you can have everything you want. God is not a genie, but God does promise to work ALL things out to our good. **Read Romans 8:28,** remember my life verse.

Chapter 3
Learning the Art of Contentment

From a book titled, *Calm My Anxious Heart* by Linda Dillow she discusses a prescription for contentment. Yes contentment plays a big part in our stinkin' thinkin'. If you're not content with your lot in life then you will complain.

The prescription for contentment is:

1. Never allow yourself to complain about anything-not even the weather.
2. Never picture yourself in any other circumstances or someplace else.
3. Never compare your lot with another's.
4. Never allow yourself to wish this or that had been otherwise.
5. Never dwell on tomorrow-remember that tomorrow is God's, not ours.

Put this prescription for contentment onto an index card and say this out loud daily. You will be amazed at how you will feel. You can have contentment in no matter what state you are in with Christ who strengthens.

> *"Not that I speak in regard to need, for I learned in whatever state I am, to be content. I know how to be abased, and I know how to abound. Everywhere and in all things have learned both to be full and to be hungry, both to abound and to suffer need."*
> *Philippians 4:1-12*

I have learned that contentment is accepting God's control over all of my circumstances. Most of us are content when are circumstances are going well, but God wants us to have contentment in all things and in all seasons in our lives.

Here is a journal entry that clearly depicts my discontentment.

8/20/05:

Sometimes the pain is unbearable. My heart aches. I am tired, and I am tired of my circumstances that always seem to get me down. I feel heaviness upon me. I feel empty and lost. I long for my child to be okay, for my family to be okay. I long to have a family I can count on. I long to have a baby and I have a hard time with others that do. I secretly want to have a child like theirs. It seems if it is not one thing it is another. This feels too heavy for me. I feel weighted down. It seems I fight every day with struggles. I have two choices, be miserable or let everything go. I can either let situations bother me or destroy me, but I am consumed by them. I have to choose to let these things go and realize I am not the one in control. I have to decide to have joy despite my circumstances. I have to surrender or be miserable. I have been through so much that I know God must have a plan in all of this. I am tired of struggling and being discontent.

Can anyone relate to this madness? Well, that was a tough season for me, but here is what I learned in that time.

1. Stop being envious or jealous of neighbors, family, friends or church members, who have what you want.
2. Stop speaking ill or gossiping about anyone. Praise God when others get blessed.
3. Stop comparing yourself to others.
4. Love everyone; love everyone right where they are at.
5. Do not be moved by circumstances or situations. Most of the time they are just temporary.
6. Do not take life so serious. Things will pass.
7. You are not responsible for everyone's happiness or contentment.

"Give your burdens to the Lord, and he will take care of you. He will not permit the godly to slip and fall."

Psalm 55:22

"But in all my distress I cried out to the Lord. He heard me from His sanctuary; my cry reached His ears."

2 Samuel 22:7

Wait for the Lord in confident expectation. Be joyful today, not when your circumstances are perfect. Enjoy your life now. Trust in the Lord with all of your heart, and lean not on your own understanding. Take comfort in the Lord, knowing he is in control. God molds, teaches and trains us through our circumstances. Surrender to Him and release all control to our Savior. Stop dwelling, pondering, wishing and wondering when, why, and where. Stop being controlled by your emotions and circumstances. Do not wish to be anybody else or have what someone else does. You really do not know what other people truly have by looking on the outside of their lives. Stop trying to force things to happen on you own time. Be content with your present circumstances. It is all about timing, and God's timing is perfect. Do not compare your situations to others; God has a unique plan for each of us individually.

"But Godliness with contentment is great gain. For we brought nothing into the world, and we can take nothing out of it. But if we have food and clothing, we will be content with that. People who want to get rich fall into temptation and a trap and into many foolish and harmful desires that plunge men into ruin and destruction."

I Timothy 6:6-10, NIV

Contentment is the atmosphere in the Promised Land where God embraces and prospers all who choose the attitudes that please Him. Contentment is a satisfaction with God's sufficient provision. Satisfied. Not needing anything else. Contentment means wanting nothing more than what God has given you.

So ask yourself now, how content are you really? Do you wish you had this family, this job, this spouse, this child? Are you satisfied with what God's provision for your life has been? I'm not saying never desire or want anything, but when that thing becomes an idol (an idol is putting anything above God) then you are risking not living with contentment.

I know all too well about this wilderness mentality. For so long, I was not truly content with my life. I had a lot of pain and heartache and I just wanted to slip into someone else's life. But you know I found out that everyone has problems and things that they go through. Yes, even that perfect little family and perfect spouse you see and want their life. Don't you know people put on masks in public and you see an illusion of their lives? Do you really know what goes on behind closed doors? So you might have a really tough, hard life but change your perspective on your life. Anything can be turned around to see that glass half full instead of half empty. What if you accepted your lot in life? Just surrender that God has a plan for your life and the things that are either in your life or out of your life are God's plans. I cannot tell you how much time I wasted wanting a different life. I really was not content with what God had given me; I had the audacity to believe it was not enough. I wanted more. I believed that I truly had legitimate desires, but they were robbing me of peace and joy. There was a time where I would have given anything to have a baby with my husband. We tried for so long and the desire was more than I could bear. I was not content with not having a biological child with my husband. I already had a son from a previous relationship when I was 16 years old, but that was not sufficient for me. I would not be content until I had this fulfilled. Do you know what I'm talking about?

Anyone ever longed for a spouse, career, children, and health? Have you ever made these things an idol in your life? I have known dear Christian sisters who have made it their top goal and mission in life to find "Mr. Perfect, Christian Husband." To my married lady friends out there, realistically is your husband perfect? Or even that fantasy that all girls dream of? I will say marriage is amazing and God's special blessing to us, BUT it is work!!! It is not what we women daydreamed about before marriage.

To the mommas and daddies out there, having your children is a gift from God, but is it as perfect as it appears on the sitcom, *The Cosby Show*? No, it is not. Parenting is hard work and it takes dedication and patience (and lots of prayer!). I thought when I finish graduate school and landed that amazing career, I will be content. Was I, No. I thought after we built our beautiful home with a swimming pool, then I know I will be content. Was I, no. I was just stubborn, I wanted what I wanted. All my dreams and desires fulfilled. Why not, I gripped; everybody else is getting their desires meet. Why not me? Ever asked yourself that question, why not me? It is a trap to keep you ensnared and tangled in deceit. God does give out good gifts and He does want to give us blessings, but He is not a genie. It does not work that way. He has an order and purpose for everything. His timing and ways are perfect, ours are not. We are human and we do not know what we really need. We always know what we want, but we don't know always what we need. Our wants are different than our needs.

Instead of talking about how big your problems are, start thanking and praising Him instead; it will confuse the enemy. Stop complaining about your life's circumstances and instead have a thankful, appreciative heart. Stop being a victim, there are many others who go through pain as well, you are not alone. Change your perspective. How do you handle life's problems? Talk about them, complain, worry, stress, and become anxious?

We have a difficult time understanding God's timing for things. We want everything on our time and on our schedule. When God is ready, He will do what needs to be done, not when we think it should be done.

Now that's the art of contentment, waiting on God's perfect time and trusting Him as we wait. Wait for God to reveal His plan. Don't take matters into your own hands either. You may be tired of waiting for a promise, a breakthrough, but remember Abraham and Sarah? They got tired of waiting on God's timing for their promised child and Sarah took matters into her own hands by having her husband impregnate her maidservant. Now ladies, does this sound like a good idea? Or does this sound like someone who got tired of waiting on God's time?

Be content with God's timing.

You are not God, so don't try and figure out a way to get your dream or desire faster. God is not slow and He does hear you. Please wait on God and don't step out of His divine will for your life.

One of the biggest lies of the enemy is that God is a cosmic vending machine. He is supposed to be my self-help genie.

Here are some key steps to take to gain contentment in your life:

1. Ask God to forgive you for wanting things your way and anything you put above Him (idols).
2. Surrender your life and your desires to God.
3. Do not worry about what you don't have. God will supply your needs not your wants.
4. Take it one day at a time. Try not to magnify everything by saying, "Oh, my life will ALWAYS be this way."
5. Allow God to transform your hurts into healing to minister to others in need.
6. Be thankful and count your blessings. Stop looking at what you don't have and what you do have.
7. Believe God is in control and HE knows best, not you!

Do you know one of our greatest desires should be for salvation for our loved ones and the people that God has put in our lives. My greatest desires before were to gain a prestigious career, have children, and a beautiful home. Now my greatest desire is that my family and loved ones would come to know Christ and serve Him with all their hearts and souls. Period. I can have everything in the world, but if my family and loved ones don't know Jesus or they are serving their sinful desires, then I really don't have what is important.

The enemy will keep you focused on what you don't have, but that is a lie, a tactic from the enemy. A scheme to cause you to be downtrodden. Stop focusing on what's wrong in your life. Get your mind off what you don't have and what everyone else does. Contentment comes from accepting what you have and not comparing your life.

Lay all of your burdens down and totally rely on the Lord. Sometimes He wants us to see that we can do nothing on our own strength.

A definition of contentment is to be calm, relaxed, and free from worry

Are you those things? If not, why? What has you discontented with life?

Perhaps you have become bitter over your circumstances or a complainer over them. I did that and I can tell you it makes it worse and not better. I wanted another life. I wanted joy and peace, and I wanted that joy and peace the Bible talks about, that no matter what our circumstances are, we can still have joy.

I just did not realize that my stinkin' thinkin' about my circumstances caused me to lose all my joy and peace and I began to wander in the dry desert. I wanted out of the desert, but I thought I had a right to complain and to be discontented continually. I thought who would not complain with all of this mess in my life. I had not made the connection that my thoughts about my circumstances were actually more important than my circumstances. My mind was in a wilderness; basically it was just plain wild. Absolutely no control, and is not one of the fruits of the Holy Spirit. Control? Well, forget that, I had no control in my thoughts. I thought about whatever I wanted and allowed whatever to come into my mind.

We are all being transformed, so keep pressing on. Focus on one day at a time. Live today, not tomorrow. Stop thinking ahead. Every day is a new day, start over every day. God's mercies are new every day. God will give you grace for each day, but He will not give you tomorrow's grace. Keep believing and know that God is always with you. Learn to smile and laugh more, it really does help. Learn from your experiences, instead of allowing them to cripple you.

Here are some true inspirational stories from famous and non-famous people. Hopefully these stories will change your perspective on your life, and you will realize you truly can be content in no matter what circumstances you have.

Ben Underwood loved to skateboard, ride his bike, play football and basketball. He learned all of these activities being blind. Nothing stopped this teenager, not even being blind at the age of 2 from retinal cancer. Both of his eyes were removed. An unflinching faith in God guided Ben and his mother during his last few months as cancer spread to his brain and spine. But while Ben was here on earth he lived with contentment. After reading about his life, how bad is your life? What are you so discontented about?

Elizabeth Murry was born in the Bronx, New York to poor, drug-addicted, and HIV parents. She was homeless at 15, when her mother died of AIDS and her father moved to a homeless shelter. She received a scholarship to Harvard University for needy students. She had to leave Harvard 3 years later to take care of her father who was dying. He eventually died of AIDS. She resumed her education at Columbia University, but she eventually went back to Harvard after his death. There has been a movie made about her life and she is a professional speaker. What if she would have said, "I want another life?" Or even allowed bitterness and anger to rob her of her destiny.

"We can complain that rose bushes have thorns, or we can rejoice that thorn bushes have roses."

Abraham Lincoln

Abraham Lincoln failed a dozen times to achieve various government offices before becoming president. What if he would have given up during the trying times and kept a sour attitude? Are you catching the theme? Its perspective and attitude.

Take for instance Charles Dickens, who worked in a London factory pasting labels on bottles of shoe polish before becoming one of the most popular authors. Imagine if he grew bitter and discontented pasting labels and just gave up.

Then there is Nelson Mandela, who spent 27 years in prison. After being released, he dedicated himself to ending apartheid in South Africa. He received the Nobel peace prize and was elected president. What if while he was in prison he said, " I might as well give up, my life is horrible. I will never get out of this stinking prison."

Chapter 4
Worry, Anxiety, and Fear: Do They Really Make Us Sick?

"So do not worry or be anxious about tomorrow, for tomorrow will have worries and anxieties of its own. Sufficient for each day is its own trouble."

Matthew 6:34

"Do not fret or have any anxiety about anything, but in every circumstance and in everything, by prayer and petition, with thanksgiving, continue to make your wants known to God."

Philippians 4:6

A definition of peace is an inability not to worry; have anxiety about; or go about in turmoil or confusion.

Dictionary.com defines worry several ways:

1. To torment oneself with or suffer from disturbing thoughts; fret.
2. To torment with cares, anxieties, etc., trouble; plague.
3. To seize, especially by the throat, with teeth and shake or mangle, as one animal does another.

Here is dictionary.com's definition of fear:

1. A distressing emotion aroused by impending danger, evil, pain, etc., whether the threat is real or imagined. Concern or anxiety. Something that causes feelings of dread or apprehension.
2. Synonymous for fear: foreboding, apprehension, dismay, dread, terror, fright, panic, horror, trepidation.

As you can see worry, anxiety and fear are all interrelated. Go back and read the definitions of worry and fear and imagine what that is doing to your physical body.

When we think worrisome, anxious and fearful thoughts, we begin to expose our physical bodies to the toxic thoughts. So what really can happen you say? A lot of well-documented research has shown the links to our physical health and our worries, anxieties and fears.

Worrying generates anxiety and reves up your body. Living in a constant state of alarm stresses your body in a bad way. Your emotional mind reacts to imaged catastrophes, as if they were real, sending signals to your body that there is a danger- a threat. Your body mobilizes to ready for the threat. People who are chronically anxious have a dramatically greater risk for developing disease including asthma, arthritis, headaches, peptic ulcers, and heart disease. Unrelenting stress compromises immune functioning and puts excessive demand on cardiovascular system. The more stress, the more likely you will catch a cold or come down with the flu. The anxiety generated by worrying keeps you in a state of disequilibrium, increasing susceptibility to a wide range of diseases and disorders.

I have worried most of my life. Now I can say that a lot of things I worried about I felt they were reasons to worry. I can say hands-down; worry, anxiety and fear will make you sick. It will drain the life out of you and you will feel mentally exhausted. My immune system was low and I just felt an overall exhaustion. Why? Because all I did was roll over in my mind the problem, analyze it from every angle, and then try and figure it out. If you are worried and anxious, this is not God's will nor desire for you. If we are really honest, why do we worry? Because we do not trust God. We are to cast our care on the Lord, not try and figure out the problems we have and create new ones that have not even happened. You might be a worry-wart if you do this. I'm not picking on you, my sister or brother in Christ, just keeping it real. Well, are you a worry-wart?

Eve Adamson in her article, *When Life is a Roller Coaster: Episodic Stress* identified several traits of a worry-wart (and you know if your worrying this much, it's going to make you sick):

1. You find yourself worrying about the things that are extremely unlikely, such as suffering from a freak accident or developing an illness.
2. You often lose sleep worrying about what would happen to you if you lost a loved one, or what would happen to your loved ones if they lost you.

You have trouble falling asleep because you can't slow down your frantic worrying.

1.   When the phone rings or mail arrives, you expect the worst possible news.
2.   You feel compelled to control the behaviors of others because you worry that they can't take care of themselves.
3.   You are overly cautious about engaging in any behavior that could possible result in harm or hurt you or to those around you, even if the risk is small.

If most of all of the statements apply to you, worry is probably having a negative effect on you. Worry and the anxiety it can produce can cause specific physical, cognitive, and emotional symptoms, from heart palpitations, dry mouth, hyperventilation, muscle pain, fatigue, fear, panic, anger, and depression.

As you can see worrying excessively really can make you sick. So what changes do you need to make in your life? Most of what we worry about never happens. Our negative thoughts and emotions are actually toxic to our physical bodies. Toxic means poison. Most people are not able to sleep at night because of chronic worry and anxiety. When you are not getting sufficient sleep at night (7-8 hours of restful sleep), your immunity can lower. I used to be so "worked up" that I had to take a prescription sleep aid to cause me to sleep. You know the sad news is, it really did not help that well, it did make me groggy in the morning. Sip some chamomile or Kava Kava tea before bedtime and give your worries and concerns to God.

Research has found that positive thinking can aid in stress management and it even plays an important role in your overall health and well-being. According to the Mayo clinic, positive thinking is linked to a wide range of health benefits including:

*   Longer life span
*   Less stress
*   Lower rates of depression
*   Increased resistance to the common cold
*   Better stress management and coping skills
*   Lower risk of cardiovascular disease-related death
*   Increased well-being
*   Better psychological health

One study of 1,558 older adults found that positive thinking could also reduce frailty during old age. One theory why positive thinking has such a strong impact on physical and mental health is people who think positive tend to less affected by stress. Another possibility is that people who think positively tend to live healthier lives in general; they may exercise more, follow a more nutritious diet and avoid unhealthy behaviors (Cherry, 2012).

Studies have shown that worry, fear and anxiety and other negative emotions weaken natural "killer cells" in our bodies. Killer cells actually attack and destroy abnormal cells. So instead, smile, that's right, smile. Why? When we smile, it sends a message to our whole body and certain chemicals are released that travel through our system relaxing our entire body and helping us to stay healthy.

I know what you might be saying, "What's there to smile about, or I don't feel like smiling." Do you have anything to be thankful for? I mean anything? Health, finances, family, job, spouse, church, a relationship with Jesus? Though your life may not be perfect, I can imagine there is something to smile about. I know that I went through periods of not smiling, but I'm here to tell you that I wasted a lot of time. My little pity-party caused me much grief. I thought at the time that I had a right to be downcast, but negative emotions and thinking will always lead you down a road that causes physical, mental/emotional, and spiritual issues and problems. Yes, there is a healthy way to grieve and go through trials and it begins with trusting God and resting in His care and His ways. Not in us controlling the universe and becoming worry-warts and control freaks.

Do you trust God? Really answer the question honestly, he already knows. This could be the beginning of your healing. Are you a worrier, full of fear and anxiety? If the answer is yes, then I'm sorry to say your trust in God is not where it needs to be. Do you want to be free, healed, and delivered from worry, anxiety and fear?

Take a step of faith and believe and pray this prayer from your heart:

Dear Jesus,

Please forgive me for not trusting you and for believing all of my worries and fears could actually change things. Search my heart and show me where I have sinned against you. I ask you Lord, to speak truth to me today. Replace all lies of the enemy and my mind with your truth. Help me to trust you and rest in your care.

Help me to take every thought captive and replace worry, anxiety and fear thoughts with trust and rest. God, show me where the enemy has been lying to me, distorting the truth. Jesus, I ask in your name, to release the enemy's strongholds from around me and to set me free. God I want to be free. Please Lord help me. Be my Shepherd and lead me to your rest and comfort. God I ask for your healing physically, mentally, and spirituality. I ask you Lord that I would sleep peacefully and restfully at night and that when I awaken you would be my first thought. Thank you for hearing me today. I praise you and I worship you.

In Jesus name

We can only have true peace through Christ. We have to practice choosing to give our anxieties to God, choose to pray specifically, choose to be thankful, and choose to dwell on the positive. We can practice these things by prayer, by faith, and by thanksgiving. It is important to maintain a posture of peace, because peace fosters faith. If you're not peaceful it is a lot easier to get upset and have your thoughts be negative.

I read an article a while back about our thinking and the effects it can have on us. The article stated that it is a scientific fact that if you go life through life in a negative state of mind, always stressed out, worried, and full of fear, your immune system will weaken, making you more susceptible to sickness and disease. Scientists have discovered that every person develops cancerous cells in their body every week. But in the tremendous immune system God has given us, we have cells called "natural killer cells." These cells are specifically designed to attack and destroy abnormal cells. Studies have shown that fear, worry, anxiety, stress and other negative emotions actually weaken those natural killer cells. In other words, if you go through life stressed and worried you will weaken your immune system. On the other hand, people who are happy and have a positive outlook develop more of these natural killer cells.

That's worth reading again. We are making ourselves sick by the way we are thinking. Do not speak fears; speak faith. Do not be anxious for anything. Do not allow fears of the unknown and the future to cause you anxiety and worry. God sees you and knows exactly where you are and what you need. Speak life over your situations and not death. Stop living in fear, waiting for the next disappointment or failure.

God tells us in His word, not to worry about tomorrow, for tomorrow will worry about its own things. Matthew 6:34. Living one day at a time keeps us from being consumed with worry. Living one day at a time brings contentment. If we saw God as the blessed controller of all things, than we would not worry because Gods plans for our lives are good and that He works everything out. Embrace today, enjoy right it where you are. Focus on what you can today, you know the popular NA/AA slogan, " take it one day at a time."

God gives us grace for today only, not tomorrow. So stop trying to live tomorrow on today's grace. Don't start to look at the future and get anxious and worried, stop!! It is not God's will that we are burdened about things we have no control over.

Most of the things we worry about never happen. Read that last sentence again.

Why do we get all worked up and stressed out? Because we believe by worrying it actually helps, we feel bad if we are not worrying. But my sisters and brothers in Christ, that is not Biblical. God says don't worry instead pray about everything. We think if we worry long enough we can solve our own problems. Did you know worry is a sin because it is not faith? When we worry we sin. I know we don't think of it is a sin when compared to adultery or murder but nonetheless, it is a sin. If you are a worry wart, then it's a sin. Repent and turn from that sin. Do not be condemned, that is from our enemy, but be convicted by the Holy Spirit.

Worry, fear, and anxiety hold hands and normally work together. Be set free and acknowledge that it is sin and ask God to help you. You will not enter God's rest with a worried and anxious mind. Trust God and then surrender your cares to Him.

Your attitude is a very important thing in your life. Life is 10% of what actually happens to you and 90% is how you react to what happens.

Chapter 5
Jealousy and Envy, Should Not Be Our Companions

I have come to the conclusion that we want what we do not have. Would we really want everything we so desired? Have you ever heard of the grass being greener on the other side? Well I believe we really think that. Have you ever caught yourself saying, "Why can't I have that?" or "I really wish I could have the perfect family." Do we really trust God completely? Does it seem He is holding something back from us or do we begin to question God? Think about that, who are we to question the creator of the universe, but we do.

Jealousy can be defined as feeling resentment against someone because of that person's success or advantages.

Jealousy has been around for as long as we can remember. It has been around since Cain and Abel (Genesis 4:1-15). Jealousy and envy are dangerous and they can destroy our efforts to love and encourage others. Jealousy is rooted in a false view of God, ourselves, and others. Basically it says, "I deserve what others have," or "God loves them better than me." Have you ever had those thoughts? Like everyone else gets the good gifts and blessings from God ,but you. When we are jealous we are telling God that we know better what we need than He does.

According to an article entitled, *Overcoming Jealousy-Causes and Cures for Jealousy*, author Karen Wolff discusses some common causes of jealousy:

I. **Unmet expectations.** Many times we place unrealistic expectations on ourselves and the people around us. If things don't happen when we think they should, we inevitably run into someone who already has want we want.

2. **A sense of entitlement**. Children leaving the nest for the first time believe their own standard of living should be the same of their parents.

3.   **Insecurity**. We can start berating ourselves for not having what other people have. Then we begin to believe negative junk about ourselves.

Wolff describes key steps to overcoming jealousy:

1.   Stop comparing yourself to others. What God has in mind for you isn't the same as for someone else.
2.   Stop wanting what other people have if you are not willing to go through what they did to get it.
3.   Stop worrying about you all the time. Find a way to be a blessing in someone's life.
4.   Start focusing on all that is positive in your life. God has given you so many wonderful gifts that many other people don't have.

Breaking free from jealousy starts with your thoughts. When you change the way you think, you change the way you feel and act. What are your thoughts about others blessings? **Everything begins in the mind first.**

"Where do wars and fights come from among you? Do they not come from your desires for pleasure that war in your members? You lust and do not have. You murder and covet and cannot obtain. You fight and war. Yet you do not have because you do not ask. You ask and do not receive, because you ask amiss, that you spend it on your pleasures."
James 4:1-3, NKJV

Jealousy can control you and even turn into hate. Jealousy is a sin and must be dealt with. If we are constantly thinking about what others have, it is a sure sign of jealousy. If you begin to blame God for repeatedly blessing someone with the things you want, you are entering dangerous territory. We may even begin to gossip and speak-ill of others who have the blessings we want. You may even have a hidden desire to see adversity come into the life of the people who have what you want. Though you may never admit this secret, God knows.

Take some time right now and ask God to search your heart for jealousy and envy. Repent and seek God's forgiveness.

"He who covers his sins will not prosper, but whoever confesses and forsakes them will have mercy."
Proverbs 28:13, NKJV

We cannot hide our jealousy from God. We can go deeper into the sin and it can destroy us. God will allow us to want in some areas of our lives to keep us faithful. Think about what you would be like if you got everything you wanted, when you wanted it and how much you wanted. Jealousy stems from selfishness and it manifest in negative speech or slander. Strife, anger, contention, slander, suspicious whispering, and inflated egos are associated with jealousy and all led to disharmony (2 Corinthians 12:20). Realize that if you have given into jealousy and allowed it to fester and grow you are giving into Satan's schemes. Jealousy is a tool of the enemy to separate people and destroy relationships.

"For where there envy and self-seeking exist, confusion and every evil thing are there."
James 3:16, NKJV

Envy is defined as feeling discontented or resentful longing aroused by someone else's possessions or qualities. A desire to have a quality, possession, or other attributes belonging to someone else.

Envy will manifest as an uneasiness and dissatisfaction with the prosperity of others. Instead of rejoicing in others blessings, you will be troubled by their blessings. Attached to envy is self-pity. Self-pity focuses on self.

Look at Genesis 37, here is a story of envy that caused pain and suffering for everyone. Joseph's brothers envied his relationship with his father. That envy led to hate and wanting Joseph dead. The Bible views envy as being very serious, even equating the gravity with murder, strife, deceit, and malice (Romans 1:29). The Bible also says in Matthew 27:18 that Jesus was crucified because of envy. Corinthians 13:4 says that love does not envy. If we truly love, we will stop envying.

Coveting is desiring something that belongs to someone else, but envy is anger towards someone for having something we do not have. Coveting produces envy and envy produces hatred. If you are not faithfully studying and walking in the Word of God, you are likely struggling with the flesh. Outwardly we can have an appearance of Godliness but inside be corrupt.

"Envy is the act of counting the other fellows blessing instead of your own."
Harold Coffinn.

"A heart at peace gives life to the body, but envy rots the bones."
Proverbs 14:30

So how does one get that level of contentment? By wanting what others have, by wishing your lot in life was different or perhaps by complaining? The answer to that is of course, "No." How do we begin to thank God for what He has given us instead of complaining? It is no easy task if you feel you been given a bunch of sour lemons, but like my grandmother would say, "If life gives you lemons, make lemonade."

We can learn so much from the apostle Paul. Turn your Bible to this passage:

> *"Not that I speak from want, for I have learned how to be content in whatever circumstance I am in."*
>
> *Philippians 4:11 NASB*

Contentment is a choice. I will say it again, contentment is a choice. We choose our attitudes about our lives. I understand that a lot of us were dealt a bad hand, but it is our thoughts towards those things that breed contentment or discontentment.

Have you ever thought about your life? If not stop right now and ask yourself what do I think of my life? Am I content? If not, why? Are you angry at God for making your life so awful? If so, talk to Him now and ask Him to help you.

Do you realize that your life is but a vapor, here now, gone tomorrow? Our lives on earth will not be forever. So what is holding you back from enjoying the contentment and joy we can have today?

Stop now and ask yourself these questions:

What are the things blocking your contentment and joy? Do you ever catch yourself fantasizing about having someone else's life?

Don't! it is waste your time fantasizing about someone else's life, this is the life God has given you.

Though it may not be what you planned or even wanted, God has chosen your life to fulfill His plans and purposes. Our lives here on earth will have pain and trouble, but God seeks to use our lives to build His kingdom. You may kick and scream, and say that it is not fair! My life sucks and if you only knew my life you would say the same. Well my dear brothers and sisters, I have had my share of relentless brokenness and heartache. So much that I will need to write an entire book just on that. I have struggled most of my life, simply not understanding why I continually had it hard and why my life has been marked by extreme pain and brokenness. I wanted a different life, plain and simple. I fought my life. Does anyone understand what I am saying by that? I would try so hard to forget my life; pretend I was someone else and even beg God to take it away. I had no idea that God was going to use every bit of my pain and hardships. I wasted so much time being discontented.

For most of my marriage I wanted a baby and we tried everything and anything to achieve this. I simply was not going to be happy until I had a baby. I was so focused on what I did not have that I failed to see my blessings. I had tunnel vision for having a baby. Now keep in mind, I did have one child but he was a rebellious teenager, not the perfect cookie-cutter family I so desired. You see when your family of origin is so dysfunctional; you begin to dream of one day having the perfect family. So my goal was to succeed at having the perfect family, and I simply would not settle for anything less. So when my rebellious teenager became even more rebellious by getting into drugs and not having a baby after 10 long years of trying to conceive, I became very discontent. Oh if I could only have so and so's life... My life would be better, so I thought. My thoughts were solely focused on getting what I thought would bring me contentment. It was a very rough time for me and that was only the tip of the iceberg, there was so much more. I became a chronic day-dreamer. Then a chronic complainer! Contentment was as far away from me as the Pacific Ocean was to me.

I learned through my rough times that ranting, raving and complete discontentment over these issues never helped. Let me repeat that, never helped. It only made the situations worse. I have learned over all these years that I have to surrender my desires and wants and trust God and to stop being jealous and envious of others blessings.

Chapter 6
Complaining, Murmuring and Whining All Lead to Thankless Hearts

A discontented life is a miserable life. There is no joy or peace in this kind of life. Do you know what a discontented life looks like? It is joyless, and it moves us to complaining, whining and murmuring. Being discontented will never bring you the life you want. But having an attitude of gratitude will. An attitude of gratitude is an attitude of thankfulness. Now we all have things we can be thankful for.

Every day write down five things to be thankful for. This will help you change your focus and be appreciative for the things you do have.

When we choose discontentment we cannot see things to be thankful for. Choose your thoughts carefully or they will devour you. So start by doing the above exercise daily and you will begin to see what you really do have to be thankful for today.

You can choose to live in the wilderness, and that just means you have not entered the promised land of Christ. In the Promised Land, it is peaceful. Do you want peace in your life? Then stop today all thoughts of a discontented life. Your life will not get any better until you choose to stop thinking negative thoughts like, "Why me, not again," or "My life has always been a disaster and it's not getting any better." These thoughts will defeat you and keep you out of Promised Land living. How long did it take the Israelites to get to the Promised Land? 40 years. It was never supposed to take that long. How long do you want to stay in the wilderness?

What would you want your life to look like? Don't hold back. What is it like? Write it down. This is an important step.

To me, having peace, joy, and contentment are the most important things to have in my life. Let's imagine for a moment having those things. Is it nice?

You most likely will experience good mental health, spiritual health and physical health. Contentment breeds health. Discontentment breeds disorder. Our circumstances can affect us negatively, if we allow them to. We have to realize that our enemy, the devil has a blueprint or a map of all our weaknesses. He studies them and brings trouble in our circumstances. He studies our reaction to these circumstances. We are wise to know our weaknesses and areas of vulnerability, because you best believe our adversary does.

> *Write out your areas of weaknesses and vulnerabilities and then be watchful in these areas. Know most likely, the enemy will attack you in your low points. He does not play fair, so you need to know your opponent's game plan.*

Be watchful in these areas of weakness, especially in times when we are sick, tired and weak. Keep especially guarded during these times. Do not be deceived, your enemy roams around like a roaring lion, waiting to devour someone. He will use your circumstances.

In my life, I usually get attacked in the same areas. I know that if I am being attacked in several of my weaknesses at the same time, I can almost rest assured the enemy is involved. We are not to engage in the enemy's schemes for us. That is where we get hooked, when we take the enemy's bait for us. We usually take the bait through a circumstance and then we begin to open our mouths and complain about the unpleasant circumstance. Have you ever said, "How much longer, I can't endure much more." Well this kind of thinking only leds to the trap of a life of discontentment. Once we fall into this trap, Satan and his dominions see that the trap has worked and will "set us up" again and again until he knows we have a stronghold or bondage in being discontent. That life always lacks joy and peace. Why? Because we are not praising our God, but shaking our fists and saying, "Our life is terrible." At this point we begin to lose our ability to be thankful. When we lose our ability to be thankful, the world is darkened. Everything looks different. We have a sour, bitter, negative attitude that stinks. We don't even really like to be with ourselves.

"Resist the devil and he will flee from you."

James 4:7 NASB

We forget that Christ has died on the cross for us and we have entered life with Him. Our focus on how everything in our life is wrong and not what is right. How can this be? Overtime our hearts become hardened if we allow thanklessness continually. Our lives are not guaranteed to be perfect and void of trials and sufferings, but somehow we expect that. I know I did or I expected the least amount of suffering possible. I honestly thought I had endured enough pain in my childhood and should now have a life free of pain and suffering. That has not happened, but God has brought me through each and every trial. I have to admit, at times I took the bait of my circumstances, and would fall into the trap of complaining and murmuring. I always tried to understand why these things happened in my life. Instead of reflecting on God's promises that He will work all things out for my good, I choose instead to reflect on self-pity and despair.

Self-pity is a victim mentality. You can be a victim of your circumstances or a victor.

"The last of human freedom is to choose one's attitude in any given circumstance."
Victor Frankl, Survivor of Nazi Holocaust

Have you ever said, "I'll be happy when...?" What a lie from the enemy. You can be content in whatever state or circumstance you are in. We have to believe that in order to have contentment.

If we say I will be content when my finances are in order, when I get married, when I have a baby, or when my children straighten up, we are fooling ourselves into believing we have to wait to be content. Contentment starts in whatever state you are in. So if you're waiting for everything to come into order to be content, stop, and start now. Don't you know it is a trap of the enemy? We will never have perfect anything. Our lives here are met with many trials and struggles, but the good news is, we can rise above our circumstances and choose to ride with Christ above the storms of life.

According to an article written by Walter Clark from the Gospel Carrier (1976), he spoke of the "subtle sin-complaining." He says that the so-called greater and more major sins are comparatively easy for the Christian to avoid. To murder someone, to steal something, even to tell a lie- all of these require definite acts of mental decision and preparation. Other sins are more subtle, and these are the ones that seem to plague Christians, in particular.

One of the most subtle sins according to this author is complaining. He discussed that to understand the sin of murmuring; we should see just what it involves in the Bible:

1. First it involves discontentment.
2. It also involves disapproval.
3. It involves discussion, particularly in the form which we regard as gossip.

4.   It involves dissension.

5.   Primarily, that the sin is often based on disbelief.

Complaining is certainly not a fruit of the spirit (Galatians 5:22-23). In fact it takes the peace and joy found in the fruit of the spirit. It squashes the fruit of the spirit by saying, "My portion is not enough or God does not know what He is doing." When we complain, we do not trust God's portion for us. We want more and we feel entitled to more. Complaining comes from unfulfilled desires, but when we trust God we can say, "His ways are best and His plans are good for me even when it does not look good." There is a lot we could complain about, but there is a lot we can give thanks about. Where is your focus?

An article by Jeremiah Burroughs entitled, *The Jewel of Christian Contentment*, he discusses that unthankfulness is an evil and a wicked effect, which comes from discontent. The scriptures ranks unthankfulness among very great sins. He says that men and women who are discontented, though they may enjoy many mercies from God, yet they are not thankful for any of them. It makes those mercies they have from God as nothing to them, because they cannot have what they want. Ouch! Anybody ever been there? I know I have. I truly did not appreciate what God gave me because I did not have what I wanted.

What we often want or ask for, is not really what we need. Only God knows our true needs, but God I want... Believe me; I have done my share of whining and being unthankful. Burroughs goes on to say that there is an evil effect in murmuring, it causes shiftings of spirit! What? Shifting of spirit? Yes, the author says, " those who murmur and are discontented, are liable to temptations to shift for themselves in sinful and ungodly ways." He discusses that there are many things you desire for your lives, and think that you would be happy if you had them, yet when they come you do not find such happiness in them, but they prove to be the greatest crosses and affiliations that you have ever had, because your hearts were immoderately set upon them before you had them. Whoa! Go back and read the last sentence very carefully.

Do we really want what we think we want? Or do we want what we think we can't have and once we get what we want, we don't want it as much? Burroughs says, " the devil is the most discontented creature in the world, he is the proudest creature that is, and the most dejected creature." So how much discontent you have, so much the spirit of Satan you have. It was the unclean spirit that found no rest; so according to this author, when a man or woman's spirit has no rest, it is a sign that it has much of the unclean spirit.

Watchman Nee is a Chinese Christian who died for his faith after decades in a communist prison, and he endured a life of hardships and heartbreaks. He had a right to complain and murmur but he did not.

Andreas Viklund from an article entitled, *Christians Should Never Complain,* says that "the reason Christians should not complain is simple: life and death are in the power of the tongue." When you complain, you rebel against God. You accuse God. You judge God. You claim that God is not being good or good enough, that He is not faithful or faithful enough, and that He is not acting in a manner according to righteousness. In the spirit realm, you are acting as a destroyer when you complain. So rather than complain and thereby bringing forth destruction with your lips, you should close your mouth so that you do not do harm. Once you stop being a destroyer with your lips, then you should do the opposite. You should praise God with your lips. You should thank God for the good.

Viklund explains that you can express your problems to God without complaining. She says we complain because we think we know better than God and that we deserve better. Ouch again! Who else is guilty of this? Just me? We are not the rulers of our lives, nor do we know best. However, we think we know best and we deserve the best.

Viklund says that complaining is a bitter fruit that comes from the corrupt seeds of rebellion, pride, vanity, selfishness, self-centeredness, boredom, fear, and impatience within our hearts.

Read Numbers 11:1, Now the people complained, it displeased the Lord; for the Lord heard it, and His anger was aroused. **Read all of Numbers 11.**

The Israelites complained and then Moses complained. God responded positively to Moses and negatively to the rest, because the people complained to one another and nothing was accomplished. Moses took his complaint to God, who could solve his problem. Many of us are good at complaining to one another, but we need to take our problems to the One who can do something about it. Dissatisfaction comes when our attention shifts from what we have to what we don't have.

The people of Israel did not seem to notice what God was doing for them, because they were so wrapped up in what God was not doing for them. They could think of nothing but the delicious food they had left behind. Are we grateful for what God has given us, or are we always thinking about what we would like to have? Our unfulfilled desires should not cause us to forget God's gifts that He has already given us. The Israelites complained all along their way to the Promised Land.

38

What has God promised you? Are you complaining because it is taking longer than expected or not happening in the manner you want?

Stop now and confess the sin of complaining and murmuring. In I Corinthians 10:10 we are exhorted not to grumble as some of them did, and were destroyed by the destroyer.

The devil actually thrives in an atmosphere of complaining. Because of the Israelites complaining and murmuring they were disciplined severely. Some of them actually lost their lives. The Israelites kept complaining that they were going to die in the wilderness, so the Lord finally allowed their complaints to come upon them. **Read Deuteronomy 8**. Are you content with the daily provisions that God has given you? Or are you becoming ungrateful for these once amazing provisions?

Author Kelly Mahoney wrote an article entitled, *What the Bible says About Complaining,,* she discussed that complaining is a sign of being ungrateful, it can lead to disobedience and you can lose sight in all the good things God does in your life. It can lead to an attitude where you lose faith and cause others to lose faith.

Dr. Dale Robbins in his article, *Complaining Only Makes Things Worse* discussed, "God dealt with the Israelites complaints as an act of unbelief directed toward Him." When they complained about their circumstances, their type of food, and even at Moses, God was displeased because they were not thankful for what He had provided for them. Dr. Robbins discusses that regardless of whatever circumstances may cause discontent, complaining is always an expression of unbelief towards God. The whole premise of Christianity is that Jesus becomes the Lord of our whole life and our circumstances. They are in His hands. Thus if believers complain, it becomes an accusation against our Lord. The Lord hears our complaints. He continues to discuss that even when the devil comes against our faith with trials that are not so good for us, God will even turn these situations around and work them together for good.

Don't become bitter and start complaining, but continue to praise God and give thanks to God in spite of all things. This will prevent the devil from overcoming you with discouragement and will send him fleeing. Thankfulness is the opposite of complaining, so give thanks instead. You might say, "Well you don't know my circumstances, you would complain too." You're right I don't know what you're going through, but I know about gut-wrenching heartache and losing everything I loved at one time. I felt like Job in the Bible at one time, and found it very difficult to find anything to praise or give thanks to God about. I was so hurt and bitter over all my loses, that I could not see anything good in my life anymore. The "dark clouds" of ungratefulness had rolled in and the sunlight was hidden. I could not get my mind around how a "good God" could allow so much pain and heartache. Whoa was me, I was having a pity-party. So when you can't see God's goodness, know He is still at work, behind the scenes. Trust Him and get rid of your bitterness.

Pray with me:

Dear Heavenly Father,

Lord, I am sorry for complaining, fault-finding and murmuring about my life. Help me to be set free today from this bondage of discontentment. Help me to give you thanks in all things. Help me Lord to be a victor of my circumstances, not a victim. Jesus, help me not to be envious or jealous of others' lives, but help me to be thankful for the life that you have given me. God, show me where the enemy has been deceiving me and lying to me in this area. Expose all the works of the enemy.

In Jesus Christ name, I pray

I recommend saying this prayer daily until it becomes a reality to you.

Here is a list you may want to copy or write out and say daily to help you become more content:

1. Stop looking back. The past is over. This is a new day and a new season.
2. Don't project the future, what it will be like or what it won't be like.
3. Focus on the day you have been given.
4. Trust God to work out your situations, don't try and figure them out.
5. Remain calm and peaceful at all times.
6. Do not complain, murmur, or fault-find
7. Do not criticize or judge others.
8. Speak faith-filled things not negative.
9. Be hopeful in all things.
10. Thank God every day.

11. Praise God continually.
12. Do not react to your circumstances.
13. Stop worrying and being anxious, instead pray about everything.
14. Do not wish your life to be different or want what others have

You can have the life you so desire. Trust God even when it looks bad, God always provides a way. The enemy always makes it look bad in the beginning and then we react and get worked-up, and there goes the trap. Pray first when a circumstance comes and be still and wait upon God. God always delivers. Do not worry about your life, don't try and figure it out, pray instead. Step out in faith, don't say, " What's the point in trying I always end-up the same way." Now that's not faith. I say try again. Try until you are completely out of the wilderness and into the Promised Land.

Chapter 7
Don't Look Back, Keep Going Forward: One Day at a Time

Do not look back; it may be a difficult season for you. You may be in the wilderness and it is time to come out. You have to get sick and tired enough of going around the same mountains. God has freedom for you; God knows our deepest longings and yearnings. Come to God who can give you complete restoration and refreshment. Do you not know that stress, worry, fear, anger, stubbornness, rebellion, and criticism do not work and it causes division between you and God? You must obey God and go with His flow. Do not live in fear anymore in dealing with others and what they could bring upon you. Believe God; believe He is more powerful than any foe or demon. Stop living in fear. If God has broken you, cheer up, because He gives grace to the humble. Believe me, being broken will humble you. God wants to pour out His spirit upon us and restore us to wholeness. Ask yourself what has broken your fellowship with God? Repent and seek God fully. He is such a forgiving God. Ask God to search your heart for any hidden sin and strive daily to maintain obedience to the Lord.

As a physician once said, "Many of my patients have nothing wrong with them except their thoughts. So I have a favorite prescription I write for them. It is a verse from the Bible, Romans 12:2." This physician does not write out the verse for his patients; rather he has them look it up themselves. The verse reads: *Be transformed by the renewing of your minds.*

Every morning before rising, say out loud, *"This is the day the Lord has made, I will rejoice and be glad in it."* Say that scripture from Psalm 118:24 at least three times before rising. When you are dressing, exercising, etc. say out loud faith-filled statements such as: I can do all things through Christ who strengthens me, I feel great physically, mentally and spiritually, I am more than a conquer through Jesus Christ. Write them out on notecards and even post them where you get ready in the morning.

William James, the famous psychologist, said, "Our belief at the beginning of a doubtful undertaking is one thing that ensures the successful outcome of your venture." Expect the best, release your faith.

Norman Vincent Peale says, " read the New Testament and select a dozen of the strong statements about faith and memorize each one. He says to say them over and over, especially just before going to sleep." Peale says in time you will have modified your thought pattern. Something else he suggests is reading your Bible for one hour every day and committing the great passages to memory and recondition your personality.

Up for a challenge? Remember from earlier you can form a new habit in 21 to 30 days, so how about trying to read the Bible every day for an hour. I know most of us would say we don't have that kind of time, but have you considered breaking that time into portions? Consider your time spent on TV watching, talking on the phone, Facebook, etc. I believe we could find the time if we really wanted to. I know we can surely find the time to do what we want, but what about investing our time in the Word of God. What if that is all we really need? *I challenge you.*

God tells us not to worry about anything, today is all you have. The things you go through are only temporary. It is how you react to them that can cause you to lose your joy and peace. The enemy will make it worse if you complain. When you praise God the enemy has to flee. Do not focus your thought on what the enemy wants you to think about. He just wants to defeat and discourage you. Trust God and do not fear, no matter the trial or circumstance. God's plans are to give you hope and a future, but the enemy's plans are to destroy. Get control of your thoughts; don't let your thoughts think whatever they would want. The enemy will have a field day if your thoughts are out of control.

In the Bible, James does not say if you face trials, but when you face trials. He assumes that we will have trials and that it is possible to profit from them. James tells us to turn our hardships into times of learning. We cannot really know the depths of our character until we see how we react under pressure. Instead of complaining about our struggles, we should see them as opportunities for growth.

Sometimes it is important to quiet our thoughts, especially during difficult times. Surrender all you think should happen. Learn to be in tune with God's voice. But you must get quiet in your thoughts first. Wait upon the Lord. God uses waiting to refresh, renew, and teach us.

"Wait on the Lord; be of good courage and He shall strengthen your heart; Wait, I say, on the Lord."

Psalm 27:14

Even those who are especially close to God as David was, have moments when they want to escape from their problems and pressures. Cast your burdens on the Lord and He shall sustain you. He shall never permit the righteous to be moved. To trust God fully means to trust Him even when we don't understand why events occur as they do. The wicked Babylonians trusted in themselves and would fall, but the just live by their faith and trust in God. Christians must trust God is directing all things, according to His purpose.

Our inner attitudes do not have to reflect our outward circumstances. It is easy to get discouraged about unpleasant circumstances or to take unimportant events to seriously. If you have not been joyful lately, you may not be looking at the right perspective.

> "Don't fret or worry. Instead of worrying, pray. Let petitions and praises shape your worries into prayers, letting God know your concerns. Before you know it, a sense of God's wholeness, everything coming together for good, will come settle you down. It's wonderful what happens when Christ displaces worry at the center of your life. Summing it all up, friends, I'd say you'll do best by filling your minds and meditating on things true, noble, reputable, authentic, compelling, gracious-the best not the worst; the beautiful, not the ugly; things to praise, not things to curse. Put into practice what you have learned from me, what you heard and saw and realized. Do that, and God, who makes everything work together, will work you into His most excellent harmonies."
>
> Philippians 4: 4-9 MSG

God wants us to come to Him with our worries and struggles. We are not to try and figure things out, analyze everything or worry. God wants us to enjoy right where we are. Don't worry about the past or the future, take hold of today. Embrace today; take it one day at a time. If something in your life has not worked out, then God has a new plan. Don't waste anymore time regretting the past or what lies ahead. That kind of thinking will lead to anxiousness and fear, and back to the wilderness you will go. Living one day at a time keeps us from being consumed with worry. Choose to give your anxieties to God, choose to pray specifically for things instead of worrying, choose to be thankful, and choose to dwell on the positives. Notice I said, "Choose." That's right we can choose to do these things. When we begin to think about tomorrow, the "what ifs," we can lose our grace for today. God gives us His manna daily, not weekly or monthly, but daily. Every day is a new day, a day of new beginnings. God's mercies are new everyday. Let each new day be a fresh start.

The Lord is in the business of teaching us, and we most likely learn the most through our problems and trails. What have you learned from your problems and trials? Do you allow God to teach you, or do you become bitter? When daily problems come our way, hold firm to your faith and don't react to the problem or situation. Don't you know that Satan watches our reactions to our problems, just hoping he can get us to get all stirred-up? The enemy wants nothing more than to steal your peace and joy, and this is usually accomplished through our reactions to our problems and trials. Try everyday to start over, it's a new day. Don't be consumed with yesterday's junk and tomorrows what if's. Don't dwell on yesterday. Dwelling means focusing on what you should have done, what you could have done and what you ought to have done. Take it one step at a time and one day at a time.

If you only had 24 hours to live, would you act differently? Well, guess what? We don't know when our time is up on earth, so stop wasting your precious time on should have, could have and ought to have.

Charles Spurgeon wrote about grace-filled Christian living. He wrote that when a man is made a child of God, he does not have a stock of grace given to him with which to go on forever, but he has grace for that day. No man of himself, even when converted, has any power except as that power is daily, constantly and perpetually infused into him by the spirit. Christians get a little stock of grace in their hands and say, "My mountain stands firm, I shall never be moved." But it is not long before the manna becomes putrid. It was only meant to be the manna for the day and we have kept it for the morrow, and therefore, it fails us. Spurgeon says we must have fresh grace. You will have grace enough for your troubles, as they come one by one.

Sometimes we think we need to see the end of our path, maybe so we can be reassured it's a good path. But God guidance is step by step. We can rest and trust that God will light our paths, one step at a time and one day at a time. Whatever comes your way, know that you can handle it, one day at a time. Don't "stockpile" tomorrow's provisions for you. Face your challenges one day at time. Don't look back at yesterday's defeats or your failures, but declare, "Today is a new day, and God's mercies are new for me every day." Looking too far down the road tends to overwhelm us in our thinking. Trusting God requires that we believe He gives us our "daily bread." Live in peace and not in anxiousness and fear of the unknown. Do you really know what is going to happen? I mean, really? We can all formulate what we think will happen, but that is called worry. Yesterday may have been troubling, but shake it off today. Remember today is a brand new day.

Chapter 8
The Physical Effects of Negative Thinking

Here is an excerpt from a journal entry from 9/10/06:

You can clearly see the effects negative thinking has on our health and mind. I wondered for so many years why I always felt bad and was always tired, it was not until I got the connection, that my thought life affected my health and emotions.

> My feelings of tiredness, apathy, and a general sense of non-well-being has stemmed from stress, life crisis and a general negative attitude. I have allowed my life circumstances to consume me. Lots of stuff happened over the past year or so and how I reacted has played havoc on my body. Infertility treatments, my son, hurricane Katrina, and my position at work. I HAVE TO LET IT ALL GO. My immune system does not work as well because of all the stress that I placed upon my body. Maybe I'm scared to release, have joy because I feel what's the point something else will happen. I have to remember things are different now, my trust and faith in the Lord has grown significantly. Are you waiting two years from now before you will experience Joy? Heal your body through renewed thinking. Stop thinking about sickness and focusing on this, even if you feel sick.

As you can see from that journal entry, my mind was a mess and so was my physical body. I never felt well and seemed to always be battling an illness. Now I know my thought life was causing most of my illnesses. Back in September of 2006, I conducted my own "experiment" to see if being thankful and positive really would change how I felt physically. I conducted this experiment on myself. In my experiment I had to for a week, choose to be positive and thankful. The conclusion from this experiment was that at the end of the week of no negative talk and being thankful, I only had two days where I felt "okay," the remaining days I felt "good." This was significantly different from what I was feeling of almost every day, "bad." Try a little experiment on yourself, even just for a day and you will see conclusively that thinking positive does affect your health and emotions.

The mind and body are linked and how you feel emotionally can determine how you feel physically. Certain hormones release hormones into the body that, in turn, can trigger the development of a host of diseases. Studies have also highly correlated emotions with infections, allergies, and autoimmune diseases. Specifically, research has linked emotions such as depression to an increased risk of developing cancer and heart disease. God never intended us to live our lives sick and diseased because of our negative thinking patterns.

75-90% of all doctor's visits to a primary care physician's office are related to stress disorders. So the question is, "What's really making you sick?" Instead of treating root causes of stress, many physicians are treating the symptoms. Prescriptions for antidepressants or antistress medications are at an all-time high. These drugs, however, do not prevent stress. Furthermore, many of the drugs used to treat stress are addictive. We have the capacity to control our thought, and we can rewire the thought patterns in our own minds and adopt new thought habits.

Psychologist, Dr. Albert Ellis developed Rational Emotive Therapy in the 1950's, he discovered that irrational thoughts, coined "automatic thoughts" can be discovered and replaced with positive thoughts. You might know this technique as Cognitive-Behavioral Therapy (CBT). God's Word tells us to take every thought captive and to renew our minds and then we will experience peace. So we can use CBT with God's word or any faith-affirming belief or statement. Basically our thoughts create our moods, so what are you thinking about?

Being a "worry wart" does not mean you are mentally ill, but it does mean you have developed a habit of worry that can lead to a neurotransmitter imbalance in the brain that can lead to a mental illness. In a lot of cases, people who worry a lot do not need medication, just a change in their thoughts. We worry because we want to control our circumstances and somehow believe we can do a better job than God. God takes care of His people like a shepherd.

"The Lord is my shepherd; I have everything I need." Psalm 23:1. What does a shepherd do?

1. He provides
2. He protects
3. He leds the sheep
4. He corrects the sheep

"Playing God" is the root of worry. We are not the shepherd but the sheep.

"Cast all your anxiety on Him because He cares for you."

1 Peter 5:7

"So don't be anxious about tomorrow, God will take care of your tomorrow too. Live one day at a time."

Matthew 6:34 (LB)

You may say, I am not worrying I am just concerned, but this can led to "overcare." What is overcare? It is being too concerned that it can lead to worry. Many clergy members experience overcare. Excessive care can turn into overcare. Many helping professions can experience overcare such as counselors, nurses and of course people in ministry work. Also overcaring can lead to not caring or ceasing not to care. Those who are taking care of their elderly parents, at the same time raising their grandchild could develop overcare.

According to an article by Fleur Hupston entitled, *Avoid the Harmful Effects of Negative Thinking* she discusses that according to experts, negativity impedes impulses from being transmitted between the central nervous system and the brain. Because the brain cannot interpret impulses correctly, this affects the functioning of the brain and body. Memory is also affected; sleep disturbances are experienced; emotional upsets become the order of the day; and immune function can also be affected, resulting in susceptibility to colds and flus.

What are some of the effects of negative thinking? According to Cristina Diaz and her article, *Effects of Negative Thinking* she discusses what the effects are:

1. Feeling down. The extent of negative feelings can go from anger, frustration, irritability, to even anxiety and depression.
2. Physical effects. The body lowers its defenses, as negativity subtracts from our energy. An extreme negative emotional state can cause eating disorders; from over eating to a complete lack of appetite and not eating enough.
3. Closing oneself down to possibilities and the flow of abundance. When we are in a negative state we do not attract those elements that would make our lives advance; rather we attract the circumstances that support us in thinking something is wrong, and we get stuck.

As you can see negative thinking does not help us but it harms us.

Here are some steps to take to help you with negative thinking patterns:

1. Offer up a sacrifice of praise to God for what you do have.
2. Think/dwell on the good things in your life and thank God for them.
3. Choose to think positive thoughts and don't accept negative thoughts.
4. Watch your words- do not speak negativity.
5. Take every thought captive, if it does not line up with the Word of God, then get rid of it immediately and replace negative thoughts with faith-filled thoughts.
6. First thing in the morning say, "This is the day the Lord has made I will rejoice and be glad in it."

Your mind must be disciplined just like you would discipline your physical body. If you want to be free of negative thinking, then you have to discipline your mind. What does that look like? Taking every thought captive, replacing negative thoughts with faith-filled thoughts, and not allowing your mind to be passive. A passive mind just allows thinking whatever it wants, and sometimes nothing at all. We have to be proactive, meaning taking charge of our thought life. The battlefield is in our minds, that's where Satan wages his war, in our minds. He plants a thought, and if you receive it as truth then a stronghold will be built. If you have a thought contrary to the Word of God and you don't accept it, but replace it with God's truth, then no stronghold can be built.

You must not allow your mind to be a garbage dump and allow Satan to dump, dump, and dump garbage. Is your mind a garbage dump? You say, I don't know,

Take the test:

1. Is your mind anxious or worried?
2. Is your mind full of negativity/pessimism?
3. Is your mind fearful?
4. Is your mind full of defeat, discouragement, and doubt?
5. Do you think self-defeating thoughts about yourself and others?
6. Is your mind critical, judgmental, or fault-finding?
7. Is your mind confused?

If you answered yes to just one of the questions, then your mind is a garbage dump. Clean your mind up, before the rottenness affects you and others. Garbage left and not disposed of properly will begin to rot and decay. Our minds, if not cleaned by the Word of God, will begin to decay. Decay means to rot slowly. Our minds left unattended to the lies of the enemy will eventually rot. We will not be transformed by the renewing of our minds, because we allowed the enemy to place whatever thoughts he wanted to into our minds. Remember, your mind is the battlefield and the enemy knows if he can defeat you in your mind, he has won the battle against you. You will feel rotten physically, mentally and spiritually from negative thinking.

If you have been defeated with negative thinking and it has begun to affect you physically, mentally and spiritually, let's pray:

Dear Heavenly Father,

We come to you today and we ask that you would forgive us for our negative thinking. Show us Lord how the enemy has lied to us. Help us Lord to take every thought captive and to renew our minds with your Word. Lord, we ask you to heal us in our bodies and minds from the effects of negative thinking. Lord, give us your mind, the mind of Christ. God, we know that we cannot do anything on our own and we ask you to deliver us from negative thinking. Help us to be thankful and to speak life and victory over our lives, the lives of others and over our circumstances. Lord, we do not want to be this way, and so we say, help. Help us Lord and deliver us out of the pattern of negative thinking.

In Jesus name we pray

"A sincere prayer brings wonderful results."

James 5:16

"You will keep him in perfect peace all who trust you, whose thoughts are fixed on you."

Isaiah 26:3

Chapter 9
Why Gratefulness is So Important

"It is not how much we have, but how much we enjoy, that makes happiness."

Charles Haddon Spurgeon

"A grateful heart is one that finds the countless blessings of God in the seemingly mundane everyday life."

Anonymous

"From a heart overflowing with gratitude, we will want to honor and glorify God by gratefully offering back to Him the many good gifts He has bestowed on us. We will not go to church to be entertained, to see "what we can get out of it" for our own private gratification, but rather to praise and worship the triune God of grace and glory."

Anonymous

What is the definition of Gratitude? Wikipedia describes gratitude as thankfulness, gratefulness, or appreciation, a feeling, emotion or attitude in acknowledgement of a benefit that one has received or will receive. The study of gratitude within psychology has only been around since the year 2000, but now psychology is recognizing the benefits on mental health . Studies have shown that spirituality is capable of enhancing a person's ability to be grateful.

Challenge:
Start keeping a gratitude journal, begin by writing 3 to 5 things you are thankful for every day.

Martin Luther referred to gratitude as "The basic Christian attitude. " Christian gratitude is regarded as a virtue that shapes not only emotions and thoughts, but actions and deeds as well. According to Jonathon Edwards, in his book, *A Treatise Concerning Religious Affections,* love, gratitude, and thankfulness towards God are among the signs of true religion. Edwards claimed that the "affection" of gratitude is one of the most accurate ways of finding the presence of God in a person's life.

> *"Oh give thanks to the Lord, for He is good; for His steadfast love endures forever! Let Israel say, "His steadfast love endures forever." Let the house of Aaron say, "His steadfast love endures forever.' Let those who fear the Lord say, "His steadfast love endures forever." Out of my distress I called on the Lord; the Lord answered me and set me free..."*
> *Psalm 118:1-18, ESV*

In an article from crosswalk.com, author Debbie Pryzbylski writes that it is not always easy to give thanks, but this is the very thing we must do in order to see God's will accomplished in our lives. This is how we move into higher realms of faith for ourselves, for our city, and for our nation. She discusses that thanksgiving breaks the power of the enemy. Whenever you give thanks to God, despite the most difficult circumstances, the enemy loses a big battle in your life. When you give thanks in the midst of difficulty, you bring pleasure to God's heart. He is looking for Christians who live in a realm of praise and thanksgiving where the enemy no longer has an ability to hold or manipulate that person. Satan is defeated when we have a thankful heart because thankfulness during difficulty is a sacrifice pleasing to God.

> *"Through Him then let us continually offer up a sacrifice of praise to God, that is, the fruit of lips that acknowledge His name."*
> *Hebrews 13:15, ESV*

> *"Give thanks in ALL circumstances; for this is the will of God in Christ Jesus for you."*
> *1 Thessalonians 5:18, ESV*

Przybylski writes that discontentment dries up the soul. David said in Psalm 116:17, *"I will sacrifice a thank offering to you and call on the name of the Lord."* Let each one of us seek to have an attitude of gratitude and thankfulness, rising to a new level of holiness. The author says you can do this by:

I.   **Thank and praise God for everything in your life.** Thank Him even for the difficulties. It is a sacrifice to do this. But He can turn troubles into triumph.

2. **Don't allow yourself to complain about anything.** During difficult times, be careful to watch your tongue, Instead of complaining, think of ways you can verbally offer God the sacrifice of thanksgiving.

3. **Don't compare yourself with others.** Don't wish that your life was different.

According to an article from the great Bible study.com, the author discussed that an unthankful heart is found in somebody who does not appreciate the things God has given them. Each one of us has been given more than we will ever know. Unthankfulness is looking at the negative, despite the positive.

Here are some symptoms of an unthankful heart:

1. People who are unthankful will naturally have negative personalities, find it easy to complain about little things, or easily become moody. Their minds are not deeply rooted and grounded in a positive or thankful pattern of thinking, therefore when something comes up that pushes their buttons,

    they .quickly forget about the goodness of God and begin to complain and grumble in their hearts. This brings about a negative personality or mood.

2. Unthankful people are known to be bitter, or unforgiving towards themselves or others. If a person is bitter or holds things against others, than it shows us they are unthankful for what God has done for them.

3. Unthankful people are always looking down on themselves or suffer from low self-esteem. We have been created in the very image of God and when we see ourselves as failures, we are in turn being, unthankful for the person God has made us.

4. Unthankful people are never satisfied with what they have been given, but always want more. We become greedy when we think about things we don't have, rather than things we do have.

5. Unthankful people don't take care of the things God has given to them. Those who are thankful for the good things God has given

them will take good care of them, whether it is their mind, body, car, spouse, children ,etc.,

A thankful heart can change the way you see your life. It is a flood-gate opener to blessings, joy and peace.

Psalm 100:4, *"Enter His gates with thanksgiving and into His courts with praise. Be thankful unto Him, and bless His name."*

"We tend to take all the gifts and pleasures and happiness and the joy without saying much to God. We take our health and strength, or food and clothing and our loved ones, all for granted; but the moment anything goes wrong we start grumbling and complaining and we say "Why should God do this to me, why should this happen to me?"

How slow are we to thank and swift to grumble."
Martin Lloyd-Jones

"Feeling gratitude and not expressing it is like wrapping a present and not giving it."
William Arthur Ward

"We would worry less if we praised more. Thanksgiving is the enemy of discontent and dissatisfaction."
Harry A. Ironside

Rev. Bruce Goettsche expressed in an article about "being grateful in good times and bad" that when tragic times hit, there does not seem much to be thankful for. Are we supposed to give thanks for the heartache? Are we to give thanks for the devastation? His answer is, "No, It is okay to hurt and to confess our pain and anger." What God wants us to do is confess that He is good. There are many things to give thanks for in the midst of heartache.

- We give thanks for a God who is working beyond the circumstances.
- We give thanks because we affirm, trust, and yes, even celebrate, the character of God.
- We give thanks for a sure hope beyond the grave.
- We give thanks for the savior who made this hope possible.
- We give thanks for a supernatural strength to get through devastation. We give thanks for a God who really does understand our pain.

"If anyone would tell you the shortest, surest way to happiness and all perfection, he must tell you to make it a rule to yourself to thank and praise God for everything that happens to you. For it is certain that whatever seeming calamity happens to you, if you thank and praise God for it, you turn it into a blessing."

William Law

Webster's dictionary defines Ingratitude as: Forgetfulness of, or poor return for, kindness received. It can also be defined as not appreciating what you have. Unexpressed gratitude is ingratitude.

Have you ever felt unappreciated by someone? How did it make you feel? How do you think God feels when we don't show Him appreciation for all the wonderful things He has given us freely? Sometimes we take our good gifts for granted. You must never take anything for granted. To God, an ungrateful heart is sin. The murmurings and unthankful attitudes condemned the Israelites from every seeing the Promised Land, and God caused them to wander in the wilderness for 40 years. We can wander in the wilderness in our minds. Are you tired of being in the wilderness with your thinking? Ask God to show you what has caused you to stay in the wilderness and then get out and stay out. We will discuss in another chapter how to stay out of the wilderness.

The Gospel of Luke records a miraculous healing of Jesus. "And He entered a certain village, there He met ten lepers that were there, which stood afar off: and they lifted up their voices, and said, Jesus, Master, have mercy on us. And when He saw them, He said, "Go show yourselves to the priests." And it came to pass, that, as they went, they were cleansed. And one of them, when he saw that he was healed, turned back, and with a loud voice glorified God, and fell down on his face at His feet, giving Him thanks: and he was a Samaritan. And Jesus answering said, "Were there not ten cleansed? But where are the nine? There are not found that returned to give glory to God, save this stranger. And He said unto him, Arise, go your way: your faith has made you whole."

Luke 17:12-19

Only one of the ten lepers returned to thank Christ. Just one. Let's look at where this ungratefulness stems from- Satan himself. Satan's heart was filled with arrogance; he was ungrateful to God for giving him life. He was not grateful to God for creating him, so he rebelled against God. He choose to believe he was better than God and that his ways are better than God.

Are we not seeing that in our culture today? So many think they know better than God and rebel against Him and His ways. Satan try's to deliver this same attitude to us. Remember Israel's example. They grumbled, complained and had ingratitude because they were afraid of being unable to overcome the

56

"giants" they saw. But these attitudes kept the Israelites from the Promised Land. What kept the Israelites from the Promised Land was not the "giants", but their ungratefulness. An entire generation died, except two men, Caleb and Joshua. Why did these men not die and enter the Promised Land? They did not grumble, complain or become ungrateful when they saw the "giants" in the land, but instead they choose the believe God.

"But know this, that in the last days perilous times will come: For men will be lovers of themselves, lovers of money, boasters, proud, blasphemers, disobedient to parents, UNTHANK-FUL, unholy."

2 Timothy 3:1-2, NKJ

One reason people turn away from God and become corrupt is because of not be thankful.

Although they knew God, they did not glorify Him as God, nor were THANKFUL, but became futile in their thoughts, and their foolish hearts were darkened. Romans 1:21, NKJ. The root of ingratitude is pride. Someone who is not thankful thinks they deserve more or they are responsible for all that they have. Nebuchadnezzar was one of those people. **Read Daniel 4:28-37.**

So you may say, "What do I have to be thankful for?" I know that type of thinking because I used to think that. I had so much hardship that I could not see what to be grateful for. Satan had blinded my eyes to my blessings and had me convinced I did not have things to be grateful for. I was bitter at the circumstances in my life and could not see what God had blessed me with, because I did not have this or that. Where is your thinking on your blessings? You might say, "I don't really have anything to be grateful for." Really? Take a deeper look, your health, family, friends, job/finances, church, family, your home, car, and your salvation? I could list so many more. Stop right here and list your blessings? Thank God for His provisions in your life. He is the sustainer and provider of your life.

Being grateful is a choice. So you may have been let down in life, but God has mercy on us and He promises to work all things out for good for those who love Him and are called according to His purposes (Romans 8:28).

"But know this, that in the last days perilous times will come: For men will be lovers of themselves, lovers of money, boasters, proud, blasphemers, disobedient to parents, UNTHANKFUL, unholy."

2 Timothy 3:1-2, NKJV

Does the above scripture describe what living in this time is like? One reason people turn away from God and become corrupt is because of not being thankful.

"Nor murmur, as some of them also murmured, and were destroyed by the destroyer. Now all these things happened to them as examples, and were written for our admonition, on whom the end of the ages have come."

1 Corinthians 10:10-11, NKJV

"Because, although they knew God, they did not glorify Him as God, nor were THANK-FUL, but became futile in their thoughts, and their foolish hearts were darkened."

Romans 1:21, NKJV

God always welcomes a thankful and grateful person into His presence. Thanks should be given to God. True sincere thanksgiving and a heart of gratefulness is pleasing to the Lord.

"Oh, give thanks to the Lord, for He is good! For His mercy endures forever."

Psalm 107:1, NKJV

Get to the root of why you are not grateful. Pride is usually the root. Have you ever said something like, "If I were God, I would do things differently." Are you resentful of God's creation? God already knows, so go ahead and admit this and repent. I was abused when I was younger and had a lot of trials growing up, so I developed an ungrateful attitude because of what happened to me. When we give thanks it keeps bitterness and hatred from taking root. Gratitude is a mark of spiritual maturity.

Here is an acronym to help you with remembering why to be grateful:
God is pleased when we are grateful
Required by God
Attitude of thankfulness is pleasing to the Lord
Thankfulness leads to God's blessings
Every good gift is from God, be thankful
Fruit of our lips, sacrifice of praise
Unthankfulness will led you into the wilderness
Lifted in spirit when we are grateful

Chapter 10
Fault-finding, Judging and Criticism are All Roads that Take You into the Wilderness

Why do we find fault with others? Is it because we believe we are better somehow than they are. God is not pleased when we find-fault and criticize others. What are our thoughts towards people? Are our thoughts gracious, forgiving, and loving, or harsh, rigid and not forgiving? Some of us were raised with parents who were critical and judging. If you were, then it is likely some of that nastiness was passed onto you. How do you know? Look at your attitude and thoughts about people who make mistakes, sin, or just annoy you. Do you think thoughts like, "I would never do that, or act that way?" Are you hypocritical of others, meaning you judge and condemn the faults of others but do not recognize your faults? We are to look at our own faults first before looking and judging the faults of others.

People who have perfectionistic qualities also suffer from being critical. Those with perfectionism, feel others should act and behave the way that they do. However, that is unrealistic to expect others will behave and act in a perfect way. People with this trait see the flaws in others, but rarely do they see their strengths. Why? Because that is how they see themselves. Grace is not extended to themselves, so grace is not extended to others. They give no room for mistakes and imperfections of any type. This can stem from childhood or having a faulty view on God's grace and mercy towards us.

Stop right now, and ask God to show you the root of your fault-finding, critical attitude. Ask God to cleanse you and forgive you. It is not your duty to be everyone's Holy Spirit. If you have not received God's grace and love, stop now and ask Him to show you His grace and love towards you. We are all in need of a Savior and none of us are perfect. Only Jesus Christ is the perfect Lamb of God. Who are we? Humble yourself, and ask God today, to remove your critical and fault-finding spirit.

Do not speak critically of your brothers and sisters in Christ. We must encourage and edify each other, not speak condemnation. When we are critical of others, we play God's role of judge. Yes we are to judge sin, but in love. I repeat in love. How many churches, Pastors and other Christians, do you know condemn with their words instead of graciously and lovingly leading that person into repentance and renewed relationship with Christ. Oh, dear sister or brother in Christ how better we would be if we would allow God to be the judge of people's hearts. How do we really know someone's heart and why they do what they do? When we speak over someone's life, we have the power to speak life or death into that person's life. What are you speaking over people's lives? You might say, "You don't know how they are behaving?" No, but God does.

When you find-fault with someone, you are actually find-fault with yourself. What we find-fault with others, is usually what we don't like about ourselves. I know you may feel it is your job to point people's flaws out, but it is not. We are not to expose another's flaws and sins through gossip, God hates gossip. We are not to use prayer as a way to gossip about others and point out their faults. Watch what you say about others and what your intention is. Is your intention to help or to point out faults and weaknesses? Dear brothers and sisters we are commanded to love, not to tear each other apart with our words.

What or who do you find fault with? Why? Who do you criticize? Why?

Don't you know you not only affect the person you are talking about negatively, you also affect yourself negatively. When we elevate our status to God and judge of people, we have committed a grave offense to Christ. The enemy is the accuser of the brethren; we should not be. Ask yourself, I'm an accuser of the brethren? Don't play with the tools that the enemy wants to destroy others' lives with, including your own. Don't you know the enemy wants to divide and destroy, and what better way than to use our mouths to pronounce judgments over people.

"Why do you criticize and pass judgment on your brother? Or you, why do you look down upon or despise your brother? For we shall all stand before the judgment seat of God. And so each of us shall give an account of himself-give lifted blame and pass judgment on one another, but rather decide and endeavor never to put a stumbling block or an obstacle or a hindrance in the way of a brother."

Romans 14:10-13, Amplified Bible

Go back to the above scripture and slowly read Christ's instructions.
The Merriam Webster Dictionary defines criticism as, an act of criticizing; to judge as a critic; to find fault; to blame others or condemn.

Jesus said, "How can you think of saying, Friend, let me help you get rid of the speck in your eye, when you can't see past the log in your own eye." (Matthew 7:4-5). Jesus is telling us the only way to understand the sin of someone else's life is to deal with the sin in our own life.

Look what Jesus said in John 8:7, "if any of you is without sin, let him be the first to throw a stone at her." This scripture is referring to the adulterous woman caught in the act of adultery and the ones who cried out, "stone her." But Jesus said, "You throw the first stone who is without sin." Guess what? No one threw a stone. So, who are you throwing "stones" at? Look at your own life first and let Jesus cleanse you and purify you. Get your eyes off others, don't you know you have enough for God to deal with.

"Do not judge, lest you be judged. For in the way you judge, you will be judged; and you by your standard of measure, it will be measured to you."
Matthew 7:1-2, NASB

Don't criticize others and don't judge others, Jesus says. Don't impose your standards of righteousness on others. We become self-righteous and holier-than though when we do that. We are all at different levels on our spiritual journey. Don't judge someone else's walk with the Lord. Extend grace to others. Grace is unmerited favor, something we did not earn. Christ does this for us, now we give that grace to others. Do we deserve to be forgiven? No, but we have been through Christ.

Allow others the freedom that Christ gives us. Don't you believe He will convict and discipline the ones He loves? You might say, "Yes, but they keep doing the same things over and over again." While that may be true, you can encourage that person, pray for that person, and gently led that person back to Christ, but you are not to impose your judgments upon that person.

When my son confessed to me about his homosexuality several years ago, my first reaction was not loving and gentle, but condemning and judgmental. I could not understand how he allowed this to happen in his life. It was not until I heard his story of how he got where he was that I stopped judging. We really don't know what somebody goes through unless we walk in their shoes.

Seek first to understand, instead of seeking to be understood. I thought it was my Christian duty to point out to my son how wrong this was and what the consequences were. I shut out all opportunities to be a witness to him and his partner. I believe one of the best things we can do for people is to seek to understand them and hear their story; however, I was not open to hearing my son's story for a while. I know God was not pleased with my attitude of judgment. I needed to look at all of his strengths and he had many instead of his sin. I was looking at the sin not the person. We all have sin, it is just this particular sin is obvious, but how many of us have secret sin? I failed to love him without "beating" him over the head with my thoughts of why it was wrong.

For parents and loved ones who have family members struggling with homosexuality, please don't push them away with condemnation. Yes, we must stand for truth and holiness but not judgmentally. How do you know your acting judgmentally? Do you say things like, "I would never do that, my walk with the Lord is strong," or "That is the worst sin." In God's eyes, sin is sin. Why do we think we know which sins are greater and bigger? Cleanse yourself first from sin and all hidden sins before making such judgments against people.

We must restore people back into the Kingdom, but only if they are ready. Why do we think we can make them righteous and holy? If they choose to stay in their sin, then dust your feet off and move on. Do not stay and continue to judge them or condemn them. You can still love people in their sin. I know you think, "That's hard." But Jesus died for the sinner and He did not love them any less.

So who are you judging, finding-fault with? The unwed pregnant teenager in your church, the woman who had an abortion, homosexuals, the homeless, prostitutes, even your spouse and children? I had an opportunity a couple of years ago to serve Thanksgiving lunch to the homeless in my community. I got to go into their "camps" and serve them lunch. Some of these "camps" were deep in the woods. How the Lord changed my views on the homeless that Thanksgiving. I always had preconceived notions about the homeless, "I know why they are homeless, they are lazy, they are on drugs and alcohol, and they don't have desire to do better." Those terrible judgments I made came to a full circle when got to meet them and spend time talking to them about their stories, it was incredible. Some had alcohol and drug addictions, but most were thankful people who knew Christ as their Savior and had terrible experiences that resulted in their homelessness. One man was walking 5 miles to a potential job he wanted to work. Another man lost everything one year, his wife and his home due to hurricane Katrina and no insurance and no extended family to help. Stop and listen to people and their stories and get rid of all preconceived notions about people. How easy it is to judge and look down on people, and speak things about them we really do not even know. "Oh, I could never end up homeless." Really? "I could never end up an extra marital affair."

Well, don't assume you know why somebody does what they do. And to my dear brothers and sisters in Christ, do not speak ill of your brother or sister in Christ who has fallen into the trap and snare of sin. Gently restore them and pray for them instead of talking about them to anyone who will here. Here is an example of what we well-meaning Christians do when we find out of someone's sin, "Can you believe she was caught having an affair?" And then we go and tell their sin to anyone who will hear. Beloved in Christ, that is wrong and we must not spread another's sin to others. If our actions are not motivated by love than our motives are wrong. Our desire should be to see that person restored to Christ not beat up and condemned. We are to be imitators of Christ. Ask yourself, "How would Jesus act, what would he say?" Jesus did not come to condemn, but to reconcile ourselves to Him. Why should we be any different?

In order for us to judge justly, we would need to know everything about that person, including their circumstances and inner thoughts. That is impossible, only God knows a man's heart. Be careful on judging peoples motives unless you can see inside their heart.

We tend to exaggerate others faults to make ourselves look better. It makes us feel superior. We don't feel quite as bad about our faults and weaknesses. We should strive to look at the good in others, and not their faults. Every Christian has areas where they need to grow, even mature Christians. We have to give people room to grow, as we have been given that same room to grow.

> *"Let no corrupt word proceed out of your mouth, but what is good for necessary edification, that it may impart grace to the hearers."*
>
> *Ephesians 4:29, NKJV*

We should not nit-pick each other. We should relax and be who God has created us to be. Most of the time we don't judge people for false doctrine, but for personal convictions. We must allow people to have their own convictions with the Lord. Do not play the Holy spirit in someone else's life.

If you judge others and are critical of others, you are in danger of your walk with God and it could hinder God's purposes for your life. Our expectations of others can lead to a critical attitude. When others fail us and don't live up to our expectations, we can begin to judge them.

"For judgment is without mercy to the one who has shown no mercy. Mercy triumphs over judgment."

James 2:13, NKJV

When we judge others we hide our own hypocrisy. Instead of judgment, extend God's love to those around you. If you are ready to criticize someone, see if you deserve the same criticism. Let's be discerning rather than negative, and desire to see people restored not torn down.

If you have been a fault-finder, a false judge of others motives than lets pray to God to help and forgive us:

Dear Heavenly Father,

We ask that you search our hearts and cleanse us of secret sin. God forgive us for fault-finding and being critical of others. God, I know it is not our place to judge others, please forgive me. Help me to love others the way you love others. Help me to see others the way you see them. Lord, rid us of critical spirits in the name of Jesus. Help us to receive your grace and love so that we can extend it to others. Lord, purify our hearts and help us to get the "log" out of our own eyes, before we try and get the speck out of others' lives. Heal us Lord from our need to judge others. Open our eyes today Lord, to what you are trying to tell us.

In Jesus name

Chapter II
Practical Steps to Keeping Your Mind out of the Wilderness

What a journey the wilderness is. For some of us the wilderness journey has been years and for others, the journey has been a short while. So have you read enough so far that you want to change your thinking? Have you seen the consequences of having a wilderness mind?

Are you ready to enter the Promised Land? It all starts in your mind and in your thinking.

Joshua remembered how discouragement at Kadesh-Barnea brought 40 years of wilderness wandering to the children of Israel. Forty long years all because they focused on the giants in the land and forgot all God had promised to them. The Israelites believed the negative report of the twelve spies instead of Joshua and Caleb's positive report (See Numbers 13-14).

These giants kept the Israelites from believing that God could overcome these human obstacles for them. After hearing this bad and negative report, Caleb speaks out and says, "Let us go up at once and take possession, for we are well able to overcome it." (Numbers 13:30).

What do you speak when you see "giants" or human impossible things in your life? This decent into the wilderness all began in their minds, what they thought of. They chose to begin to think negatively about God and His promises and began to complain and grumble. It is only a matter of time, if we do this that our minds will become a wilderness.

A wilderness mind does not have the mind of Christ, but it is unstable and confused.

What does your mind look like? Is your mind full of garbage and lies?

Is it at rest and enjoying peace? If you believe the report of the "giants" in your life instead of trusting God for His promises, you will not enter the Promised Land. So what are the "giants" in your life? What are the things you complain about, and that you are negative about because the circumstances are difficult? Are you able to thank God for your trials or do you feel angry and bitter towards God? Why do we thank God for our trials? Because through them we gain endurance and our character is developed. God also promises to work all things out for our good if we love Him.

What have you believed? The report of the enemy or of God?

What have you spoken about your circumstances, other people, yourself?

Be strong and courageous my sister or brother in Christ and speak what God has said and believe His report. Everything begins in your mind and then if you accept whatever comes into your mind as truth, you will next speak it out, and lastly you will begin to behave that way. The enemy knows this and he starts putting lies into your mind, so that will begin to speak those lies out.

Write down the "giants" in your life and start speaking God's promises over them, even if you can't see what God is doing. I promise He is doing something. Rise up and begin to see that if you are defeated in your mind, then you are defeated in your walk with the Lord. Do not fear the schemes and the distortions the enemy shows you. The enemy magnifies and enlarges our problems, and when we begin to speak negative over our problems, the enemy knows he has and can defeat us. There is power in our words. Choose to speak faith over your circumstances. The enemy does not know your thoughts, but he does know what you say out loud. The enemy will set you up so that you will react and start saying what you see instead of what God has promised. Go and pray before opening your mouth about something. Watch your words, for they will be used to increase your faith or decrease your faith.

If you have gone into the wilderness because of your thinking, the first thing you want to do is repent. Repent of all things you have spoken or thought that you know God did want from you and repent of all secret sin. Ask God to show you all sin that is hidden from you.

Get completely cleansed of all sins. Though you may have thought, "oh, worry or doubt is not that big of a deal," still it is sin. Sin is sin to God. Forgive others and let go of every offense you have towards anyone, including God. That's right, God. Search your heart and see if you are upset with God for the things that have been allowed in your life. Are you believing that if you were God you would have done things differently in your life? *Tell God how you truly feel, He already knows.*

Stop now and have fellowship with God. Tell Him how you don't understand and that you are disappointed, but that you will choose to trust Him anyhow. Ask God to show you all the lies Satan has brought into your mind. An example would be, "God is not fair or God does not really love you because He would not have allowed all this pain in your life." Replace all the lies with God's truth over every lie. Remember that is how Satan works by getting us to believe a lie. It started in the Garden of Eden with Eve, when Satan said to Eve, "Did God really say you could not eat from the tree of good and evil?" Eve took the bait and believed the lie. Just because something sounds right does not mean it is right or truth. It might "feel" right to say, " God does not see me or hear me because nothing seems to change." The reality is God does see and hear us, but He works on His perfect Divine timing. So we might "feel" that is truth but our feelings are deceiving. Always believe the truth in God's word.

God is forming you to be the kind of person who can overcome giants through faith in God. The Israelites could have been out of the wilderness in two years if they had believed God's promises for them. Those who meditate on God's word are preparing for God's blessings and promises. Those who tolerate sin are preparing themselves for painful dealings. Even if our bodily desires are not satisfied, we should still give thanks. Is it not the goal in life to be like Christ not fulfill all of our desires? Even when you are tempted to grumble against God and complain about things, choose to have faith and believe God will move you to better things.

People often get what they say (Proverbs 6:2; Mark 11:23). If despite your trying circumstances, you continue to believe and confess the promise of the Word of God for your life you are sowing seeds for a great harvest of blessings. If you believe in God's faithfulness and mercy, and desire to please Him, you will come into better things. When we complain we are saying to God that he is not doing right and that He is not fair and just.

Keep in mind that before God decided to take the children of Israel into the Promised Land, He first decided to test them by keeping them out in the wilderness for about 2 ½ years. Could you consider that the things happening in your life are a test if you would remain faithful? What if you could get to the Promised Land living a lot quicker if you remained faithful and trusting to God? A faith not tested, is not faith at all. How do you know you really have faith unless it has been tested?

We may sometimes wander if God will ever respond to our prayers, but we must never give up hope or doubt. At the right time He will respond. Christ did not come to take away challenges, but to change us on the inside and empower us to deal with problems from God's perspective. Satan tempted Eve by getting her to doubt God's goodness. Satan made Eve forget all that God had given her and instead, focus on the one thing she could not have. Are you focusing on something you want and believing God is not good because he has not given it to you? Have you forgotten all God has done for you and remaining fixated on the one thing you have not received?

Our goal should be to face suffering as Christ did, with patience, calmness and confidence that God is in control of the future. We can say we trust the Lord, but He wants to see the fruit of it. Here is a part of my journal entry that shows my wilderness mentality and God's response to it.

Remember early when I said to talk to God about how you feel because He knows everything, well that is what I did. You can see how genuine I was with the Lord.
9/7/10:

Dear God,

I love you and I am thankful you are here and that I am not alone. Lord, I trust you. I believe you are working all things out for good. Please draw near me and bring me strength. God I pray you will deliver me from worry, anxiety, fear, doubt, people approval, and guilt. Lord, please help me to have unshakable faith and to trust in you. I believe hope has been deferred for me for so many things, and I have found fault and complained over my lot. Lord, could you help me to be content in all things? Lord, could you help me to never to judge, criticize, find fault, gossip, or be negative? Can you help me to love others the way you love others? God, help me out of this pit. Could I please not go around these same mountains again? Could you please show me why I keep going around the same mountains over and over again? Lord, show me how to be thankful always and to praise you in all things.
This was God's response to me:

My child, you have finally gotten things. For so many years, we have been working on the same issues. It did not have to take this long but I will use everything. I love you, I am for you, and I will show you the way. You know the power of words now. I will deliver you from all of these things, but it is up to you to keep them out. Stay out of the wilderness by praising me and having thankfulness.

As you can see I had stayed in the wilderness a long time. I did not have to stay that long but I choose to see the "giants" in my life, instead of believing what God had promised. My mind was in the wilderness for about 7 years.

For a while I felt justified in my negativity and complaining because I had so many trials and a lot of pain. When my mind became a wilderness, it started out with how I perceived what was going on in my life and how I reacted. Both of my grandparents died back to back to one another and both suffered in the end, my parents divorced after 35 years in marriage, and realizing that I was not going to have a baby with my husband and undergoing fertility treatments and surgeries. This was the beginning of my decent into the wilderness.

I began to complain, compare my life to others, become negative, and believe that God did not have goodness for me. You see I began to believe the lies of the enemy, because I had already had such a troubled childhood. I believed that I did not deserve anymore pain and suffering. I felt justified complaining because I felt I had already endured so much. If I would only not have seen the "giants" in my life and believed the report of the enemy, I believe I would have come out of the wilderness sooner. But I didn't, and more pain was heaped upon me. My only son began to struggle with drug and alcohol addiction and is placed in three different treatment facilities, he still continued to struggle. I also became aware that he was living a homosexual lifestyle. I was completely devastated and believed the evil reports of the evil one, and began speaking hopeless and faithless things over my life and his, I became so bitter and disillusioned.

Meanwhile, I still am unable to have a child with my husband; it has been 10 long years. I became very bitter with my life. I was also dealing with several other family members who were dysfunctional and drug addicted. So I felt everything was being ripped from me, and I spoke of how I felt. I spoke what I saw, not what God was saying. He kept telling me to wait, hold on, He is working things out, and to be patient. But I didn't, and I wanted anybody's life, but mine. I choose to see all the "giants" in my life and I reacted to them, just like the Israelites did. What did Joshua and Caleb do though? They believed they could conquer the giants. Choose carefully what you speak out when you are undergoing trials, because your enemies hear you, and I believe they magnify your circumstances.

Over the past 7 years of my wilderness mentality, I believe the following steps God gave me to stay out of the wilderness. I believe if you follow these steps you to could have freedom to enter the Promised Land. I encourage you to write these out on a notecard and say them every day, as a reminder to you. Speak these steps out loud.

Practical Steps to Staying out of the Wilderness Mentality

1. Do not worry about anything.
2. Enjoy your life.

3. Don't compare yourself to others.
4. Don't judge, criticize or find-fault.
5. Do not complain or grumble.
6. Watch what you say and think-speak faith-filled words.
7. Replace negative thoughts immediately with the truth of God's word.
8. Pursue and maintain peace. Be at peace with yourself and others.
9. Do not be fearful. Do not live in fear.
10. Do not worry about what others think of you.
11. Do not be bound by guilt or shame- I have forgiven you and set you free.
12. Have faith and do not doubt, no matter what it looks like.
13. Forgive offenses immediately. Be forgiving.
14. Be hopeful over every situation and circumstance, regardless of how it looks.
15. Do not react in anger by your words or behavior.
16. Trust God even when you don't know what will happen.
17. Don't analyze or figure things out.
18. Be thankful and rejoice always for everything.
19. Have a heart of praise.
20. Be full of joy despite your circumstances.
21. Do not please man, but God.
22. Do not speak or think negative.
23. Do not react to circumstances, but remain calm and come to God and pray and believe He hears you and is working it out.
24. Do not be jealous or envious of others.
25. Be content with what you have.
26. Rest in God, even when difficulties happen.
27. Love yourself and do not speak negative over yourself.

Take it one day at a time.

Chapter 12

How Do You Know You Are Out of the Wilderness?

So you might be thinking what it would look like if your mind was out of the wilderness. There are some key things to look for as your clearing your mind of wilderness thinking. I hope that you have seen over the chapters what a wilderness mind looks like and the physical, mental and spiritual effects a wilderness mind can have.

Let's go back to the beginning of the book, it usually takes 21-30 days to break a habit or form a new habit. With God's help it could be sooner, but don't get discouraged if takes longer or you have to try several times.

Don't give up, be determined that you will not live your life defeated. Your mind is what's holding you up from freedom. That's right your mind, your stinkin' thinkin'. So don't get discouraged if you are not where you would like to be. Remember how long you have been this way; it takes time to change. Be determined though you will not give up and give into old patterns of thinking.

It's up to you now. Do you want to live in freedom? It's your choice. You can choose to live defeated and negative or move into the promised land. It will take work and lots of dedication, but you can do it; It is so worth it.

Ask yourself these questions:

1. Are you fearful?
2. Are you worried or anxious?
3. Do you react negatively to your circumstances?
4. Do you doubt and not trust God?
5. Are you judgmental? A fault-finder?
6. Are you a complainer?
7. Are you jealous or envious of others?
8. Do you think negative about yourself and your circumstances?

9.   Are you grateful and appreciative?

10.   Are you content with your life?

If you answered yes to just one of the questions, your mind is in the wilderness and you cannot enter into the Promised Land like that.

You must by faith, believe that God is working in your life and the life of others and begin to think and speak not of the "giants" in your life, but of the promises of God. It takes faith to enter the Promised Land. If your mind is a wilderness, one that is doubtful, critical, complaining, negative, you need to clear out the brush today in your mind. Pull away everything in your mind that does not support faith and hope. You might think, "What's the point,? I have already tried before." Then, try again. Failure is only failure when you stop trying. Do you want to live faithful and hopeful or discouraged and defeated?

Life change takes place when you change how you think.

Do you want a changed life? Your life cannot change until your mind is under the control of Christ. There is no other way. You can have great intentions for your life, but if your mind is a mess you will not get very far. Take control of your thoughts and stop every thought that is not of faith or hopeful.

"Whatever things are true, whatever things are of noble, whatever things are just, whatever things are pure, whatever things are lovely, whatever things are of good report, if there is anything praiseworthy-meditate on these things."

Philippians 4:8-3

The apostle Paul knew the importance of programming our minds with thoughts that are true, noble, just, pure, lovely, of good report, virtuous, and praiseworthy. Anything else that comes into our minds must be rejected and replaced immediately with the truth of God's word. If not, your mind will became a wilderness and you will be confused and doubtful, not living a life a faith.

You might be thinking, "You don't know my life, I have a right to think negative." Your right I don't know your life, but I can say from experience that thinking anything less than faith and hope for your life, will keep you in the wilderness.

That is a long list, but I believe if you follow what is on the list in obedience and faith, God will move you from the wilderness in your mind. God is moved by our obedience and faith in Him, nothing else.

So are you sick and tired of your life? Tried doing things your way, and you're not getting any better? Get out today of the vicious cycle of doing things like you have always done.

Surrender your life right now, to the one who can transform your thinking and give you His mind. If your mind is looking through a negative filter at your life and circumstances, than you will experience a faith-less life. A life with no power, no victory and no freedom.

It does take some time to exchange your thoughts with God's thoughts, but it is important that you take it one day at a time. If you don't get it right one day, than get up again and try again. You can experience what God has for you when you align your thinking with His thoughts.

When you experience an exchange of your negative thoughts with what God thinks about you, you will experience God's peace, joy and hope.

Your circumstances may or may not change, but your perspective about them has and when you change your perspective you receive an outpouring of God's peace, joy and hope.

You can waste your entire life being fearful, anxious, worried, negative, and critical, or you can live your life in hope that God is in control and He will work out for our good what bad things have come into our lives. So do not get impatient while you are waiting on God to work out those things for good, instead praise Him and thank Him that he will work it out.

Once again, I can almost hear your thoughts, "What is she talking about, does she know what I am going through, praise and thank God for what?" Been there, and I can tell you one thing, being thankless never helps.

Stop right now and begin to thank God for what He has blessed you with. You want to come out of the wilderness mentality, don't you? Then, begin today thanking and praising our Lord and Savior for His blessings in your life.

If your mind is cluttered with negativity, thanking God will seem strange and it may seem unnatural, I say, "Do it anyways." Eventually, when you praise and thank God without a push or it feeling unnatural, you know you're out of the wilderness. Don't look at the "giants" in your life, those things that are in your life that are difficult and trying. If you look at the "giants" in in life before thanking and praising God, you will never do it.

When you feel hopeful again, you know you're not in the wilderness mentality.

You feel a sense of hope that flows naturally and you even feel hopeful over the "giants" in your life. Before, the "giants" overwhelmed you and caused you to shriek back in fear and worry, but now you're looking to God to cause good to come from those things. You don't know when or really how He will do it, but you know He will. Hope is the cornerstone of your life, it overflows in every aspect of your life. You can't contain it, and even want to share it with others. Before, you had no hope, so you could not give away something you did not possess yourself. You wanted to give hope to others, but you lacked trust and doubted God was going to do anything in your situation.

I was in the wilderness for 7 years, now that's a long time. My mind was a wilderness. I was living a hopeless, defeated, discouraged life, with no victory. The enemy penetrated my mind and his deadly assaults ambushed me. I did not take every thought captive. I listened to the lies of the enemy; I played his "tapes" over and over in my mind, until they eventually erected strongholds in my mind. You might be wondering, "How did the enemy take over your mind like that, I mean were you not a Christian?" Yes, I was, but I had some heavy circumstances come into my life and I felt God was not answering my prayers and had abandoned me. I begin to believe the lies of the enemy over God's truth, but I thought I was being punished for receiving all the hardships that I had.

Can anybody relate to what I am saying? Have you ever been so crushed by life's circumstances and you call out to God and there is silence! So, for 7 years, I decided to side with the enemy on what he was saying about my life and circumstances. Before long, I was experiencing depression, insomnia, anxiety, fatigue, headaches, sickness, irritability and anger.

Doctors could not help nor diagnose the problem because it was not a physical problem but a spiritual problem. I began to get into holistic, natural medicines. I started eating good, exercising and taking herbs and vitamins. While, I am a huge advocate for holistic healing, my problem was that my thinking and thoughts were literally making me sick. I could not believe that just some random, " jacked-up" thoughts I would have could cause me to be sick, tired, depressed and angry. So, even though God was telling me my problem was not my circumstances but how I thought about them that was causing me to feel bad. I continued anyhow, to think and believe whatever came into my mind. Well, eventually I got so tired I could not get out of bed in the mornings and felt an overall sense of not feeling good. I was very frustrated that I did not have a cold, flu, allergies, something I could figure out and diagnose, but I began to feel an overall sense of malaise. I did not know what was wrong, so I upped my intake of vitamins and herbs. However, it did not work. I was such a skeptic on believing our thoughts affect our moods and behavior. I thought, once again, "There just thoughts, how are they harming me?" I finally had enough one day. I could not get out of the bed and I was feeling hopeless and depressed, again! I got sick and tired of living this way. I had finally come to the end of my rope. I thought I would ask God that He would reveal to me the source of my fatigue and depression and maybe He could heal me. But once again, The Lord reminded me it was my thinking and thoughts not my circumstances that were causing me to feel bad. I thought, "Well, I can listen to God this time or go back to what I am doing."

We know the definition of insanity: doing the same thing over and over again, expecting different results. Well, I was not going to be insane again! Enough, living in this bondage. I got really serious with the Lord, and asked Him, "What do you want me to do, and I will do it this time!" The Lord showed me that I was to start disciplining my mind. I could no longer just let anything come into my mind and accept it as truth, I had to take every thought captive.

The Lord also wanted me to start thanking and praising Him, even though none, and I repeat none of my circumstances was any different. Okay, now that last one was a bit much for me, since I had become accustomed to being a complainer, grumbler and a whiner about my circumstances. I thought, I deserved to be able to complain about my circumstances because they were so horrific. I am not exaggerating either, my circumstances were beyond what I thought any human should have to endure. I felt very justified in my complaining, so thanking and praising God when I was in grief, upon unresolved grief, was a bit much. You may be asking what unresolved grief is, I know what grief is, but not unresolved grief. I believe unresolved grief is harder to overcome, because there is no end to it.

An example of normal grief, is death of a loved one. You can eventually make terms with the fact that your loved one is not coming back on this earth and they (hopefully) will be united with Christ. But unresolved grief is finding out your only son is living a homosexual lifestyle and your unable to have any more children. How can you properly grieve these things? Very difficult, because unresolved grief cannot be "buried" anywhere. You can't come to terms with a death per se, because there was not really a death, but you learn eventually you have to grieve the "death" of a dream or desire. When I was hit with back to back grief, my thoughts turned bitter and negative. Well, "How can Suzie Q, who is unmarried have yet another baby she can't afford." Or thoughts like, "Why can't my child be superstar Christian like that family at church." My thoughts were disturbing. I was angry, and I doubted God's goodness. Why did I doubt God's goodness, because the enemy told me that," If God cared about you, He would not let this happen to you, and God really does not love you, everybody else He loves but you."

How horrible I allowed a vulnerable time in my life, to turn me against what God thought of me. Friends in Christ, let me say this, "God does love you and He is not trying to harm you and keep things from you." Do not believe the lies of the enemy. He will plant all sorts of deception in your mind about God. Trust God even when you cannot see the outcome. I had to eventually do that; that was one of the best decisions that I have ever made in my life. I had to fight at first for my mind. Once Satan has a stronghold in your mind, he does not give it up easy. I say fight, anyway. I am a living testimony to God's restoration and redemption. Yes, because I was obedient and stopped believing the lies the enemy was giving me and I began to thank and praise God for my blessings,

He supernaturally changed my perspective about my life and my circumstances. Praise Jesus, I am free.

You can have that too! God is not a respecter of persons, which means He will do for you what He did for me. The key though, is lining your thoughts with His, and praising and thanking Him while you're waiting for your victory. I promise if you are obedient to what God has directed you to do, He will cause you to be more than victorious. Yes, you will have to take a step of faith. Let me repeat that again, you will have to step out in faith. What does stepping out in faith look like? Believing God and trusting God even when you can't see what He is doing or even if He will do anything.

Take a chance and believe that God will bless your obedience to take a step out in faith. This is a reality, most of my circumstances have not changed. What has changed are my thoughts about them. I know have peace, joy and hope, despite my circumstances. Also, I feel really good physically. I do not feel that overall sense of not feeling well. I am able to get up in the morning well rested and not fatigued. Depression and anxiety have lifted and I am not as irritable and angry as before. Turns out I had just been looking through dark-colored glasses instead of the lenses God wanted me to look through.

There is a peace that has come on me that has nothing to do with my circumstances. I really don't know when my circumstances will change, or if ever, but I am content that God is control. I know that God will cause everything meant to harm me to work out for my good, so I rest in that. I have surrendered the control to try and figure out how all of my circumstances will work out. I take it one day at a time and I recognize that God's grace is given out daily for my problems. The problem before, is that I wanted His grace for my problems for my lifetime. Sorry, it does not work that away. God's grace is sufficient for each day, not in advance.

You would dare to believe God again? I know if you are like me, you may be saying, " I did believe God before and He let me down." Friend, I truly know how you feel. It is pretty bummer to feel let down by our Father in heaven. Would you try again to believe, once again? I know how difficult it can be to get up and hope again.

Let me ask you this though, "If you don't hope again, than what?" The truth is when you don't hope, you really do not feel like living. That's the truth, death actually looks better than living this life.

My brothers and sisters in Christ that is a lie straight from the pit of hell. **If the enemy can't kill you physically than he will try and kill your hopes, dreams, love for God, and your purpose for your life.**

If you don't have hope, you then begin to lose your purpose for living. What a horrible cycle to be on, and just think it all begins in our minds. As said before, the battlefield really is in our minds. So that is why Satan attacks your minds like he does, and believe me he is relentless. He studies you and sees your reaction to things, and then he will plant suggestions in your mind for you to take as bait. If you take the bait (his lies), he will hook you. Think of it like a fisherman who baits his fishing pole. This lure or bait is usually sparkly and it moves attracting fish that come by. If a fisherman baited his hook with nothing, the fish would just swim away noticing a large hook instead of some attractive lure. That is how Satan gets us, he shows or tells us about some fancy "lure," and if we don't exam that "lure" properly we will swallow the "lure." What happens after swallowing the "lure?" It gets lodged in our minds like a hook, and removing this "hook" becomes very difficult. So, don't take the bait. The bait most likely will come disguised with the truth and a lie behind it. All sin and temptation starts in the mind. This started with Eve in the Garden of Eden. Satan said to Eve, "Did God really say you can't eat from the tree of good and evil?" Eve thought about this lie and the thought eventually became an act.

This is worth repeating again, everything we do starts in our minds.

Every affair, every act of violence, every bad attitude, every addiction, and every act of disobedience starts in the mind with a thought.

This is why this book is so important. Please go back and read it again, underline, highlight and meditate on what is in this book. This is no ordinary book; I believe this book was a Divine inspiration from God and that if you are reading this, it is not a coincidence.

If you have picked up this book it because God is trying to tell you something. Please listen to what God is saying to you in this book.

Let us pray together:

Father,

We thank you for this day and all you have blessed us with. Would you show me how the enemy has been lying to me and distorting my perception about things. God, would you help me to learn to be thankful and to give you praise despite what I am going through. Would you cause good to come out of the harm that has come into my life. Help me to wait on you and your promises and fill me again with hope. God, help me to get right with you. Search my heart and cleanse my heart. Lord, let me be obedient to you and your ways. Please help me to trust you and to hope once again. God show me who you really are and I pray that I will have true intimacy with you. Help me to take every thought that comes into my mind captive and to renew my mind with your truth. God give me faith to see where I cannot see. Open my heart again to you and work out your will in my life. God I pray that you would bless me with your presence, your peace, your joy and your hope. God, I want to be on fire for you. Set me on fire for you and let your hope in me overflow to others. God let your spirit fall on me today and let me not be the same again. God, what do you want me to do? To change? Give me the strength and power to do as you ask. God help me to be obedient to you. Lord, please change my life, I can't, but you can. Lord, I ask all of this for you today believing you can do all these things. I wait with expectation and anticipation.

In your Son's precious and Holy name, Jesus.

Conclusion

Are you ready for a changed life? Really, are you ready? Then let's review how to stay out of the wilderness. It starts in your mind, you're thinking.

Do you have stinkin' thinkin'? Stinkin' thinkin' is like a poison toxin to your spirit. *You are what you think.*

I know it is not easy to change your mindset, but it can be done with Christ giving you instruction and direction. The wilderness mentality is dry, barren and fruitless. Nothing can be harvested or produced on this dry and barren land. If a poison toxin is in your mind, can a poison toxin produce anything? No, it can't, poison kills. Kills what you say? Your dreams, goals, walk with God, relationships, health (both physical and mental), and self-esteem. Negativity is like poison to your soul. "Drink" enough of this poison and it will eventually "kill" you.

Christ wants us free in all areas of our lives and that includes our thinking. You cannot have a life full of negativity and a life full of positivity; the negativity will eventually take over. So you must choose which one, and sometimes you have to choose daily and even hour by hour. It is a choice. You make life what you want it to be. I know what you might be saying, " You just don't know my life." Well, guess what, you don't know mine either. I have shared brief parts of my testimony throughout this book, but there is so much I did not tell.

I wanted this book to reflect more on God's goodness then the hardships I faced. I can reassure you, I understand pain, crisis, fear, devastation, grief, and trials. I have had my fair share of them. But my thinking and attitude about my life had always been to complain and to want another life. I was upset with God and thought he was upset with me. I thought I got the "raw" end of the deal in life. I really thought that. I have learned that it is not my circumstances that need to change, it is my thinking about my circumstances that needed to change. Things will happen and are going to happen. We cannot control life, but we can control our reactions to what happens in our lives.

To have a radical paradigm shift in your thinking is no easy task.; the enemy will try and discourage you. You may hear things like, " Just give up, you will never change." That is a lie. Discern lies from truth immediately. You must replace the lies with the truth of God's word. Even if you don't feel like it and are agreeing with the lie.

Praise and a thankful heart will help you not have a wilderness mentality. There is always something to be thankful for. Look around at your blessings and thank God for what you do have and not for what you don't have. Change your perspective. Look at things differently. See the good in a situation not the bad. I am sure you can find good an any situation, it may be a little difficult, but try. Don't always focus on the negative of a situation. Turn the situation around, and see the good that is in it or can come out of it. We sometimes make mountains out of molehills. God is in tuned to a thankful and grateful heart. It grieves God when we complain and murmur about our lives. So change your perspective.

Remember, you may not see instant results. Change can be a process. Don't give up and quit if you are not seeing results immediately. Keep going.

You may get this process quicker than I did, but however long it takes be determined to see it through. It will be worth all of your time and efforts. God has a plan and He will not stop working on you, unless you refuse His intervention. Let God do His work and you cooperate with His plan.

Now let's us think for a moment what your life would look like in the Promised Land.

That means your thoughts and mind are faith-filled, positive and encouraging. Your new life would have these characteristics: peace, joy despite your circumstances, hope, faith, and complete trust in the Almighty God. Imagine that for a minute. Sounds impossible or not realistic? I know, I thought so too at one time. But really, these traits all could be in your possession. Even if your circumstances are still difficult and trying.

Do you believe? You might say, "Truly, no." It's okay, but don't stay there.

Stop right now and ask God to help you believe and to fill you right now with His hope. It is okay, He already knows your heart.

Write out what you would like your life to look like. Write your hopes, dreams, and prayers to be answered. Pray over these things but then believe that God heard you and He will in His time. Do not engage in worry, fear, or doubt over your circumstances. What does worry change anyhow? Also, write down all the areas of your thinking that need to be changed. Become aware of those areas and then ask God to forgive you and help you to overcome them.

Be of good cheer, for God has overcome the world and you through Christ will overcome your wildness mentality. Believe. Receive. God is not a respecter of persons, what He has done for me, He will do for you.

Are you sick and tired of your mindset? Then if you are, take the lessons from this book and APPLY them to your life.

If you do not apply what you learned and just read the book, it will be of no value.

You may need to read the book first and then go back and read it again applying each concept, one at a time. Underline, highlight, and journal what stuck out for you in the book, put certain things that pertained to you on note-cards and reread them often. This is how you begin applying what you have learned. If you just read the book and do not apply the principals, you will not gain the full impact of this book.

Notes

Chapter 1: The Habit of Positive Thinking

1. Norman Vincent Peale, *The Power of Positive Thinking* (Prentice Hall Press, 1987).
2. New King James Version, *Life Application Study Bible* (Tyndale House Publishing, 1996).
3. Joyce Meyer, *The Battlefield of the Mind* (Warner Faith, 1995).
4. Kendra Cherry, *What is Positive Thinking?* http://www.psychology.about.com/od/PositivePsychology/f/positive-thinking.htm (assessed February 2, 2012).
5. Fleur Hupston, *Avoid the Harmful effects of Negative Thinking*, September 26, 2010, hhtp://naturalnews.com/z029850_negativity_thinking.html (assessed April 10, 2010).
6. The NASB Message Parallel Study Bible, (Zondervan, 2004).
7. Drs. Henry Cloud & John Townsend, *Boundaries* (Zondervan, 1992).

Chapter 2: So What is Wilderness Thinking?

1. Personal journal entries taken from May 4, 2005 & August 5, 2005.
2. Various Christian music artists: Hillsong, Martha Munizzi, Juanita Bynum, Third Day, Mercy Me, Grits and Lacrae.

Chapter 3: Why is it so Important to Learn to have Contentment?

1. Linda Dillow, *Calm my Anxious Heart* (NavPress, 1998) Pg. 11-12. Permission given to use pgs.11-12 from book, the prescription for contentment by NavPress.
2. Personal journal entry from August 20, 2005
3. New International Version Bible (Zondervan Publishers, 1984)
4. Inspirational stories from Ben Underwood, Elizabeth Murray, Abraham Lincoln, Charles Dickens and Nelson Mandela. All inspirational stories can be found by internet search using their names.

Chapter 4: Worry, Anxiety, and Fear: Do They Really Make Us Sick?

1. Dictionary.com, *Definition of Fear*, (assessed February 2, 2012).
2. Dictionary.com, *Definition of Peace*, (assessed February 2, 2012).

3.   Dictionary.com, *Definition of Worry*, (assessed February 2, 2012).
4.   Eve Adamson, *When Life is a Roller Coaster : Episodic Stress*, http://www. netplaces.com/stress-management/stress-unmasked/when-life-is-a-roller-coaster *(assessed February 2, 2012)*.
5.   Kendra Cherry, *What is Positive Thinking?* http://www.psychology.about.com/od/PositivePsychology/f/positive-thinking.htm (assessed February 2, 2012).

Chapter 5: Jealousy and Envy, They are Not Our Friends

1.   Karen Wolff, *Overcoming Jealousy-Causes and Cures for Jealousy*, http://christianity.about.com/od/overcomejealousy/a/positivethinkin.htm.   (assessed February 2, 2012).
2.   New King James Bible, *Life Application Study Bible* (Tyndale, 1996).
3.   NASB and The Message Parallel Study Bible, (Zondervan, 2004).

Chapter 6: Complaining, Murmuring and Whining All Lead to Thankless Hearts

1.   NASB and The Message Parallel Bible, (Zondervan, 1994).
2.   Walter Clark, *Complaining the Subtle Sin*, Winter 1976-77 http://www.hi-rock.com/complain.html (assessed February 28, 2012).
3.   Jeremiah Burroughs, *The Jewel of Christian Contentment*, http://www.monergism.com/contentment05.html (assessed February 28, 2012).
4.   Andrea Viklund, *Christians should Never Complain*, http://healthand-devotionalarchieves.wordpress.com/category/christians-should-never-complain.com (assessed February 28, 2012).
5.   New King James Version Bible, (Tyndale, 1996).
6.   Kelly Mahoney, *What the Bible says about Complaining*, http://www.christianteens.about.com/od/advice/f/complaining.htm (assessed February 28, 2012).
7.   Dr. Dale Robbins, *Complaining Only Makes Things Worse*, http://www.victorious.org/complain.htm (assessed February 28, 2012).

Chapter 7: Don't look Back, Keep Going Forward: One Day at a Time

1.   Norman Vincent Peale, *The Power of Positive Thinking*, (Prentiss Hall Press, 1987).
2.   NASB and The Message Parallel Study Bible, (Zondervan, 2004).
3.   Charles Spurgeon, *Grace-Filled Christian Living: One Day at a Time*, http://www.erictyoung.com/2011/03/28/grace-filled-christian-living-one-day-at-a-time (assessed April 4, 2012).

Chapter 8: How Does Negative Thinking Really Affect Us?

1. Personal journal entry from September 10, 2006
2. Fleur Hupston, *Avoid the Harmful Effects of Negative Thinking*, September 26, 2010, http://www.naturalnews.com/z029850_negativity_thinking.html (assessed April 10, 2012).
3. Cristina Diaz, *Effects of Negative Thinking*, http://www.the-benefits-of-positive-thinking.com/effects-of-negative-thinking.html (assessed April 10, 2012).

Chapter 9: Why Gratefulness is so Important

1. Debbie Przyblski, *Thanksgiving: The Power of a Thankful Heart*, November 16, 2009, http://www.crosswalk.com/special-coverage/thanksgiving/thanksgiving-the-power-of-a-thankful-heart-11616835.html (assessed January 24, 2012).
2. English Standard Version Bible (Good News Publishers, 2007).
3. Rev. Bruce Goettsche, *Being Grateful in Good Times and in Bad*, November 19, 2000, http://www.unionchurch.com/archive/111900.html (assessed January 24, 2012).
4. Wikipedia.com, Definition of Gratitude.
5. Websterdictionary.com, Definition of Ingratitude.
6. New King James Version Bible, (Tyndale: 1996).

Chapter 10: Fault-finding, Judging, and Criticism are all Roads that Take You Into the Wilderness

1. Amplified Bible, (Zondervan Publishers, 1987).
2. NASB and The Message Parallel Bible, (Zondervan, 2004).
3. New King James Version Bible, (Tyndale, 1996).

Chapter 11: Practical Steps for Staying out of the Wilderness

1. Personal journal entry from September 7, 2010.

*All inspirational quotes given throughout the book were taken from http://www.dailychristainquote.com.html and http://www.hopetriumphant.com/thanksgiving_quotes.htm

Appendix A: Affirmations

Instructions: Write out these affirmations on note cards and add or change any affirmation that may or may not apply to you. Say these affirmations at least once a day, preferably twice a day, once in the morning and before bed.

I. You are not a failure.

2. You are a jewel in God's kingdom, a rare treasure.

3. You have been anointed with gifts to serve God.

4. You have great worth and value.

5. You have confidence because of Christ in you.

6. You are a warrior. You are bold, courageous and brave.

7. You are lovable and you love others the way Christ loves you.

8. You are being refined for God's service.

9. You are compassionate.

10. You have a heart for the hurting.

II. You have determination and a strong-will. You do not give up easily.

12. You are free to love and not live in fear.

About the Author

Stephanie holds a Masters of Social Work from the University of Southern Mississippi and is a licenced social worker. She also has a bachelor's degree in Psychlogy. She is a Licenced Belief Therapist through the Therapon Institute and is a Board Certified Christian Counselor through the International Board of Christian Counselors. Stephanie is a member of the American Association of Christian Counselors, and the International Society of Mental Health Online.

Stephanie counsels women through her counseling ministry, Hope Ministry. Stephanie is also an author, speaker, and teacher. She has recently begun online counseling for women. She also teaches Bible studies, support groups and mentors young women. Stephanie continues to write and speak when requested.

Stephanie lives in Biloxi, Mississippi with her husband, Stephen of 15 years. They have one dog Gizmo and a doggie angel in heaven, Kobe, who passed away while writing this book. They have one grown son, Jonathon.

Please let me know how this book has helped you.
To contact Stephanie through her website,
www.christianhopecounseling.com
email at: stephanie@christianhopecounseling.com
Twitter @StephRReck
Facebook.com/Hopecounselingminsitry

Made in the USA
San Bernardino, CA
26 August 2013